REMNANTS OF OUR PAST

DEIRDRE O'NEILL is the creator of the Remnants of Our Past project, using various social media accounts to satisfy her own huge interest in Irish heritage, history, arts and crafts. She is married with three children and this is her first book.

A donkey carrying seaweed, An Cheathrú Rua, County Galway. (Photograph by Kathleen Price © National Folklore Collection, UCD.)

The STORIES of our ANCESTORS hidden in the IRISH LANDSCAPE

REMNANTS OF OUR PAST

DEIRDRE O'NEILL

GILL BOOKS

Gill Books
Hume Avenue
Park West
Dublin 12
www.gillbooks.ie

Gill Books is an imprint of M.H. Gill and Co.

© Deirdre O'Neill 2025
All photographs © Deirdre O'Neill except where otherwise stated.
978 18045 8247 3

Edited by Jane Rogers
Proofread by Anna Kealy
Designed by Graham Thew © Gill Books
Printed and bound by L.E.G.O. SpA, Italy
Typeset by Padraig McCormack
This book is typeset in 10.5pt on 16pt, Calluna.

The paper used in this book comes from the wood pulp of sustainably managed forests.

All rights reserved.
No part of this publication may be copied, reproduced or transmitted in any form or by any means, without written permission of the publishers.

To the best of our knowledge, this book complies in full with the requirements of the General Product Safety Regulation (GPSR). For further information and help with any safety queries, please contact us at productsafety@gill.ie.

A CIP catalogue record for this book is available from the British Library.

5 4 3 2 1

To my husband Steven, who explored these ancestral trails by my side and whose deep support and encouragement made this book possible. To my children, for their insightful critiques and Irish language input. *Go raibh míle maith agaibh.*

CONTENTS

Introduction 9

The Household 11
Food and Drink 12
Washing Day 20

The Village 27
The Forge 29
Horses 38
Bridges 47
The Pound 52

The Sea 59
Fishing 60
Seaweed 69
Salt 75

The Land 83
Cattle 84
Rundale 88
Travelling Labourers 92
Reliance on Potatoes 96
Lime 101
Milling 108
Iron 116

The Fun of the Fair... **125**
The Fair Day... *126*
The Pattern Day.. *132*
Faction Fighting... *137*

Pastimes **147**
Handball.. *148*
Stone Lifting... *155*

Cures **165**
Stones.. *166*
Water... *175*
Trees... *187*
Blessed Clay.. *195*
Sweathouses *202*

Death... **209**
The Wake.. *210*
The Burial.. *212*
Keening *222*
Undertakers... *223*
Memorials... *226*

Afterword 231
Bibliography 233
Acknowledgements.. 253

Gravestone carved with blacksmiths' tools, Kille Abbey, Moorgagagh, County Mayo

INTRODUCTION

Remnants of our past lie all over Ireland, telling the story of the Irish people and their daily lives, how they sustained themselves, their beliefs and traditions, how they died and how they were remembered.

Visitors to Ireland in the eighteenth and nineteenth centuries detail the kindly welcome and hospitality extended to them by the Irish people they encountered on their travels, despite the poverty and inequity that was observed.

This book sets out to tell the story of the people who lived and worked in these old ruins. What is now a cold hearth in a collapsing fireplace was once the warm place where the family gathered and the fire was never allowed to go out. The tranquil parks in our villages were once bustling fair greens, echoing with the bellowing of livestock and the howls of faction fighters. The pretty stream that flows through a park might once have been where the women of the village washed clothes together, or where water was collected for the busy blacksmith's forge.

The story around these physical remnants, and the lives they touched, firmly grounds our knowledge in the roots of our society.

Traditional thatched house, early twentieth century (© Library of Congress)

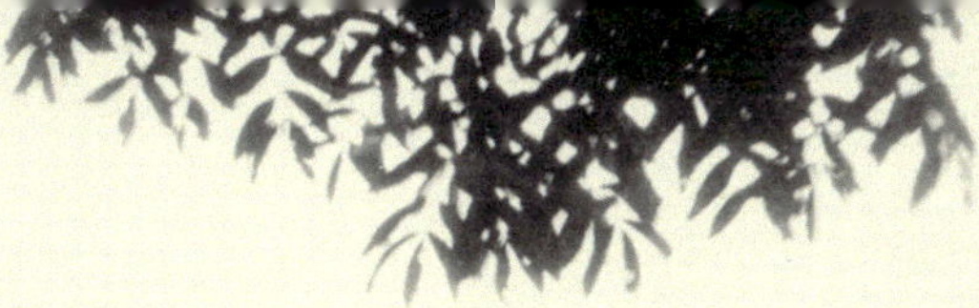

THE HOUSEHOLD

FOOD AND DRINK

Scenes of feasting and hospitality occur frequently in Irish legends that have come down to us from ancient times. Feasting was an important social custom, and in accounts of the Fianna (the band of elite warrior-hunters led by Fionn MacCumhaill), while out hunting in the summer, the warriors would roast their meat on spits and wrap other meat in straw to cook in pits they had dug.

There is actual evidence in our landscape of large ancient cooking pits, in which the people of Ireland are thought to have cooked meat. Known as a *fulacht fiadh*, a cooking pit was made by digging a hole into the earth which was lined with stone (or wood). The theory is that our ancestors filled the *fulacht fiadh* with water, usually from a nearby stream, heated stones

Fulacht fiadh, *Drombeg, County Cork*

A crane, which swung outwards, on which the heavy pots and kettle hung on pot hangers. The shelf was called the hob. (On display at the Ulster American Folk Park.)

in an adjacent fire and rolled them into the trough to heat the water. They would then drop the wrapped meat (or other food) into the pit to cook it. The advantage of boiling meat rather than roasting it was that the precious fat was also rendered and saved. We now see evidence of mounds enclosing the trough, often crescent shaped, containing burnt stones shattered by heat, along with dark soil caused by discarded charcoal and ash. In one modern recreation, around one hundred gallons of water was brought to the boil with twenty-five heated stones in under half an hour.

Thousands of these ancient pits have been found across Ireland, which mostly date to the Bronze Age (so some could have been used c.4,000 years ago). Perhaps the food for ancient Irish feasts was cooked in these pits, but *fulachtaí fia* may also have been used for other activities that involve heating water, such as brewing, bathing (also mentioned in accounts of the Fianna), rituals, metalworking, dyeing and tanning animal hides.

Cooking methods progressed and in more recent centuries, the style of fireplace in an Irish house dictated the types of food that were cooked. Most houses had only an open hearth where the fuel, usually turf (peat), was burned at floor level, with no grate or oven compartment. This meant that the fire could be divided as it burned, with smaller fires moved around as needed for the various cooking vessels. These included a pot that was called an oven that would be set on the fire, and burning embers would be placed on its lid to surround the food inside with heat. Cooking vessels were heavy, so a crane was often used to rotate them out from the fire as needed. If a metal vessel was not available, liquid was boiled in a wooden vessel by dropping hot round stones into it, a small-scale version of the *fulacht fiadh* method.

The fire was of utmost importance in the house, as it supplied the family's food, heat and hot water. The stone shelf, or hob, that was built into these fireplaces could be used for moving pots off the fire or drying oatcakes. It would become blackened from the smoke and spills and some people whitened this a couple of times a week with lime (whitewash) from a bucket kept nearby. Our modern hobs, usually referring to cooktops, come from the name of this shelf.

In many areas, potatoes were the mainstay of people's diet. When the potatoes were boiled, they were strained (or 'teemed') by pouring the contents onto a large round shallow wicker basket called a skib (or *ciseog*), through which the water passed into a second pot on which the skib sat. Since they often had no table, this arrangement then acted as table and platter, around which the family gathered. They would peel the potatoes with their fingernails and then dip the potatoes into a condiment that sat in the centre of the basket, known

Eating potatoes around a skib, c.1915. Photograph by A.W. Cutler, printed in National Geographic, *April 1915.*

A grill for cooking herring, which was placed directly over the fire. The oily herring juice ran along the channels and, having collected in the recessed well in the centre, was used to dip the potatoes for flavour. (On display at Glenview Folk Museum, Ballinamore, County Leitrim.)

as 'kitchen' or 'dip'. This took the form of salt, a vessel of milk or buttermilk, or a herring in its cooking juices – a common expression was 'Dip in the dip and leave the herring to your father.' Or there might be a 'yellow mackerel', which was a fish smoked by putting it up the chimney. After the meal, the skib was scrubbed clean and hung on the wall to dry, a sight that is often captured in old photographs of Irish houses. If the men were far from home digging potatoes, they would light a fire in the field and roast some potatoes for their meal, again peeling them with their fingernails.

People had customs to make their basic diet seem more appealing and filling. They might somewhat humorously point their potato towards butter, lard or a salted herring hanging nearby and simply imagine the taste, a custom known as 'potatoes and point'. There are also reports that they sometimes half-boiled the potatoes so that the outside was cooked and the inside was raw and crunchy. This was known as the bone of the potato or the moon (due to its ringed pattern). In 1844, just before the Great Hunger, Dr James Johnson, who had visited Ireland, theorised that the reason for this was to make the potato less immediately digestible so as to allay the 'gnawings of hunger' between meals, which consisted solely of potatoes.

Where available, oats played a part in the people's diet, eaten as porridge or ground into meal and used to bake bread. Oatcakes were also made by mixing oatmeal with salt and hot water, shaping them into discs and then placing them on stands near the fire to bake and dry out. The dried, crumbly oatcakes lasted for months and would be carried as a food supply by Irish emigrants on long ship journeys.

A one-roomed house, probably built around the late eighteenth century. Note the skib hanging on the wall and the clay floor. Three-legged pots were steadier than four-legged ones on these uneven floors, and sometimes clay was scooped out of the floor to form a hole for the pot to sit into, to steady it (to pound food in it, for example). This house was dismantled stone by stone and moved to the Ulster American Folk Park.

Griddle (left) and hardening stand (right). The griddle sat directly over the fire, and flat bread was placed on it and turned over during baking. In the eighteenth and nineteenth centuries the hardening stand (known by various other names, including harnen stand or grid iron) was used for drying oatcakes slowly beside the fire. (On display at the Ulster American Folk Park, County Tyrone.)

A great treat in the Irish house was flummery, which was made by steeping oatmeal in lukewarm water for several days, stirring regularly, then straining into a pot and simmering the starchy liquid with some sugar until it thickened. When set, flummery was a fulfilling, curd-like dish, eaten cold with milk. A sustaining drink for the men working in the fields, humorously called 'bull's milk', was made by steeping oatmeal and oat 'seeds' (the oat hulls left over after milling) for at least a few days until fermented. The result, after straining, was a sour-tasting yet refreshing and nutritious milky water. This was useful during the times of the year when cow's milk was scarce.

Bread was another staple food. One of the ways people baked was to use barm, a sweet rising agent, which they could get from a local brewery or make themselves by fermenting oatmeal or cooked mashed potatoes in water. This was useful when they were observing a black fast (a Christian Lenten fast when dairy and meat is not allowed), as it meant they didn't have to use buttermilk to make bread. Domestic ovens were not a common feature in the average house, but there is evidence that bread was available commercially from village ovens (often run in conjunction with a grocery business) and from markets, where bakers were sometimes penalised for selling 'light bread' – bread deficient in weight. A delivery system might even be offered, where bread could be delivered to the countryside by cart. In an 1844 advertisement, George Baker of Hibernian Bakery in Dublin marketed how his business could deliver bread in both town and country.

The Irish house also had tea stewing away all day, resulting in a thick syrupy drink that might even be reheated the next day. After the Great Hunger, tea became more affordable and more popular among the poor, but there are stories that when tea was first introduced people did not know how to prepare it, and they ate the leaves and threw away the liquid. One story from County Clare tells how a woman bought some tea leaves to try to impress the priest, and after boiling them, served them up to him on a plate.

WASHING DAY

The washing pool or pond was once a hive of activity and conversation, a place where groups of women eased the laborious tasks on washing day with camaraderie, catching up on local news or singing together. While some women, known as washerwomen, specialised in washing laundry as a profession for the locality, the task was also done by women for their own households.

Before houses had running water, women would gather at a source of fresh water such as a pond or a stream, rather than hauling buckets to their homes. Having steeped the clothes first, they then pounded them with a wooden mallet called a beetle (*slis* in Irish), or slapped them on a stone to dislodge dirt. The stone was called a bittling stone or a washing stone and the beating was called bittling. When the writer William Makepeace Thackeray visited Ireland in 1842, he noted women in the river near the castle in Limerick: 'Yonder you see a dozen pair of red legs glittering in the water, their owners being employed

Washing stones in Adare Washing Pool, County Limerick

*Women bittling in the river c.1830 near Old Baal's Bridge,
Limerick City, probably at the location that Thackeray described*

in washing their own or other people's rags.'

The clothes were then rinsed in fresh water, spread on a hedge or the grass and left to bleach in the sun. They would be sprinkled with water at intervals to prolong the bleaching reaction of the sun on the damp cloth. It was said that, when dry, they

'A Connemara Washing', published in The Graphic *in 1871.
Note the beetle the woman is using to pound the clothes.*

were as white as snow, but the process would be repeated if necessary. The same method was applied to bleaching textiles commercially, and the green areas where the cloth was spread became known as bleachgreens, which then

Women washing clothes, Connemara, County Galway, 1892 (© National Library of Ireland)

became absorbed into placenames like Bleachgreen (such as in Collooney, County Sligo) or Bleach Road (such as in Kilkenny City).

While clothes could be washed with water and pounding alone, other methods could be used to help clean stains and whiten clothes. Records from the 1930s tell of traditions employed 'long ago', with accounts of sheep droppings being applied to clothes, which were then left to steep (known as 'sheep's green', according to one story), or clothes being steeped in urine that had been aged for three weeks. The urine collected for this purpose was precious; one record relates that a large vessel containing urine remained unemptied in the room during the wake of a man who had died. The women could scrub the clothes with home-made soap made with fat and ashes, or they might use a peeled raw potato cut in half. If the clothes were dark, they were washed in water in which ivy leaves had been previously boiled, which prevented their natural dye fading.

The women also made starch to stiffen collars by squeezing the liquid out of raw grated potatoes through a cloth and allowing the resulting water to settle. The starch formed on the bottom and the water was changed until it remained clear, after which the starch was dried and bleached in the sun before being used. The leftover potato pulp would be used to make potato bread or pancakes (called boxty).

Monday was washing day, and it was deemed unlucky to wash on any other day. This old rhyme was recorded across the country:

> They who wash on Monday have all the week to dry
> They who wash on Tuesday are not so much awry
> They who wash on Wednesday are not so much to blame
> They who wash on Thursday wash for shame
> They who wash on Friday wash for need
> They who wash on Saturday, oh, they are sluts indeed!

(At the time, 'slut' meant an unkempt, slovenly woman.)

Two women bittling in the foreground of Jonathan Fisher's print The Mills near Chapel Izod with a distant view of Palmerston, *published in 1792*

The local tradition is that these stones were used as washing stones. Originally in a different formation, they have been moved to their current location to keep them safe. Bruff, County Limerick.

Supernatural events were associated with washerwomen. A common story in many areas was that a local holy well was so offended by a woman washing clothes in its water that it dried up and then sprang up in another location. There are also stories of ghostly women bittling clothes and then disappearing after an interaction with the human who saw them. Another one relates to the banshee (*bean sí*), a supernatural woman whose shrieking and wailing at night signals an imminent death in the family. She was often associated with washing stones, and people reported seeing her at night, bittling clothes and crying, just before a death. A similar creature in Scotland was the *bean nighe* (washerwoman) or the Washer at the Ford, who signalled a death by washing the bloodstained clothing or the shroud of a person about to die. This name has the same Gaelic linguistic root as the Irish *nigh*, meaning to wash – in Irish 'washerwoman' is *bean níocháin*. The legendary Irish warrior Cú Chulainn encountered the goddess the Morrigan washing his blood out of his armour, foreshadowing his death.

'The Song of Mary Cruise' is a ballad recounting a real-life fifteenth-century young woman who was rediscovered as an Irish heiress because she was overheard singing about her lost lands while washing clothes at a stone by the River Thames. 'Hear me sighing, on this cold stone, mean labours plying, yet Rathmore's heiress might I name me ...' Her mother had fled Ireland after her husband was murdered when she was pregnant with her daughter and they had lived in poverty in England. Sir Thomas Plunkett, an Irish man who happened to be walking by the washing stones, recognised the story in the song, represented her case, and later became Mary's husband.

The need for washing pools diminished over time: commercial washing soda became widely available and affordable, running water was introduced into houses and technology progressed, and so washing day activity moved into the home. The folklore archive recorded in the 1930s tells how people might greet children with, 'it is often your mother and my mother, bittled in the one pond'; binding generations through their work at the washing pool.

Washing stone, Milltown, County Galway, moved to a public park for preservation

A forge that operated in Bridge Street, Antrim. Note the men gathered inside.

Pikes displayed at Wicklow Gaol, where many of the captured Irish rebels were held in 1798

THE FORGE

The blacksmith's forge was a focal point in villages throughout Ireland, a place where men gathered while waiting for their turn with the blacksmith. They spent this time sharing local news, negotiating business deals in the warmth of the forge's fire and consulting the advertisements pinned to the forge door, which was often used as the local noticeboard.

During the run-up to the 1798 rebellion against British rule, forges became safe meeting places for rebels and busy manufactories of arms. The Irish rebels had little access to muskets, artillery or horses, and depended on weapons made by blacksmiths. Miles Byrne, a rebel leader, later wrote in his memoirs that pikes were 'easily had at this time, for almost every blacksmith was an

Hammond's Forge, Coppenagh, County Kilkenny, where the blacksmith Henry Hammond made pikes for the 1798 Rebellion. He was subsequently hanged publicly at Kilkenny Gaol.

United Irishman'. A pike was a long spear that could reach past bayonets, and the shape of the pike head depended on the style of the local blacksmith. Many had curved sharpened hooks (or double hooks), which were used to pull enemy soldiers off their horses.

At this time, just being a blacksmith was enough to draw the suspicion of the yeomanry (the militia loyal to the British government) and forges were often raided, with some burned to the ground. As the Patrick Archer poem 'Páid O'Donoghue' says, 'The blacksmith thought of Ireland and found he'd work to do.' But the penalty for blacksmiths caught forging weapons (or merely suspected of forging weapons) was death. Many were hanged beside their forge or at the local jail as a public punishment and warning to others. In

The plaque commemorating Henry Hammond at Hammond's Forge, Coppenagh, County Kilkenny

A forged iron gate (crafted in the forge in Clonbullogue, County Offaly) that has stood the test of time. A typical example of blacksmith-forged gates, with its flat iron bars and hot iron rivets.

fact, in the following decades, the threat of blacksmiths was closely monitored by the requirement to register all forges in Ireland.

The growth of horse-reliant agriculture, transport and trade in the early eighteenth century saw a commensurate growth in blacksmithing. The forge functioned like the modern service station, where travellers stopped to get their cartwheels and horses' hooves serviced. At a time when every village was self-sufficient, the blacksmith designed, made and repaired most ironwork, including household equipment such as fire cranes, pot hooks and spinning wheel parts, and farm equipment such as ploughs, scythes, gates and hinges. In winter, he would be busy making spade blades for the spring, with each spade taking many hours of hard hammering to make.

Often located at crossroads for easy access, these now silent forges once echoed with the rhythmic ping of the hammer on the iron and the hissing of hot horseshoes, their singeing smell mixing with that of the horse and the smoke from the fire blazing constantly in the dark. The fire and bellows were usually situated in the depths of the forge (darkness was important for the smith to judge the colour of the heated iron to see when it was ready), where sparks flew onto the anvil and water trough nearby. The horse was brought into the forge for shoeing, to the large space just inside the entrance door where the best natural light was. Before access to veterinary medicine, the blacksmith was often also a farrier, a specialist in the care of horses' feet and legs, with skills to calm the horse as the horseshoe was hammered onto its hoof. He would act as a horse doctor, with knowledge of how to care for horses' teeth

A wheel with a metal rim, its hub sitting into the hole of a binding stone, also known as a shoeing stone. Old millstones were the perfect shape to reuse for this purpose. Parke's Castle, County Leitrim.

A memorial statue of a rebel blacksmith, Páid O'Donoghue, who is remembered in Patrick Archer's poem of the same name. It tells how he made his escape from yeomen who were forcing him to shoe their captain's horse before planning to kill him. He sank his hammer into the captain's head and made his escape on the horse. Curragha, County Meath.

and treat injuries and diseases, including with herbal remedies. Blacksmiths' skills with horses, combined with their metalworking knowledge, made them in demand in the military.

Most forges were built beside a stream because water was needed for cooling hot iron. Outside the forge lay the binding stone, where a hot iron band was placed around a cartwheel, the stone's hole receiving the wheel's hub so it lay flat. Once the band was fitted onto the wheel, cold water was applied to quench the fire that the high temperature had ignited on the wooden wheel, cool the iron, and shrink it to create a tight bond.

Blacksmiths could make their own nails, but they would more often source them from a 'nailer', who made nails predominantly for horseshoeing and shoe-making. Hot iron rods were pointed and then placed in a mould and struck with a hammer to make the head of the nail. Another responsibility of the nailer was to make pigs' nose rings. His skills were so in demand that a common saying for a busy person was 'He is as busy as a nailer.'

The forge at Clonbullogue, County Offaly, built in 1866

The blacksmith Mick Silk, an expert in treating horses where others failed, imprinted his name on this forged iron gate in Milltown, County Galway. Blacksmiths often stamped their name on the flat slam bar of the gates they made.

    The craft of blacksmithing was taught to apprentices, who were indentured for several years. Strict conditions were imposed, for example not being allowed to play cards, frequent a tavern without permission, or get married. Because it was such heavy work, with some tasks (such as wheel binding) needing two people, it was also common for a blacksmith to employ a journeyman, a temporary assistant blacksmith often known as a 'striker' because their main job was to strike the iron repeatedly with a sledgehammer. Blacksmithing was often a generational craft, with fathers passing their skills to their sons, so many forges passed through many generations of the same family. *Gabha* is the Irish for blacksmith, and many of these families had names with derivatives of the word, such as MacGabhann or McGowan.

    For blacksmithing families, cash flow was a common problem. Fuel and iron had to be bought, but the local farmers would be slow to settle their

The interior of a forge, silent for many years. Note the horse ring on the wall on the right, used to secure the horse during shoeing. In the area local to this forge it was said that you could cure warts by washing your hands in the blacksmith's water trough or by stealing some of the water without letting anyone see you.

bills. It was a tradition in the community that many customers settled their bills by delivering turf to the blacksmith or doing farmwork for him, planting or harvesting his crops, thus freeing him up to work in the forge. On some occasions, the head of a slaughtered animal went as tribute to the blacksmith, a tradition going back to ancient times.

Blacksmiths were believed to bring good luck and to have supernatural powers: the power to curse and the power to cure. Turning the anvil a certain way was believed to put a curse on a person, including death, but the smith could also cure liver ailments or rickets (among other health issues), and he would physically undertake procedures like pulling teeth. The water from the forge trough, where the irons were cooled, was believed to have special qualities, including curing warts. The seventh-generation blacksmith of a blacksmithing family was thought to have particularly powerful supernatural abilities.

The local forges were recalled as fun places to be, with the blacksmith often a great storyteller who was rarely without an audience; and where groups of men gather among heavy objects, there are bound to be challenges to test each other's abilities. These trials of strength included tossing the anvil, or lifting a sledgehammer by the end of its shaft over the head, fully extending the arm and hammer. The blacksmith himself was usually regarded as the strong man of the locality, due to the repetitive heavy lifting and striking required in his job.

While the blacksmith had an important role in the community and was always the go-to person to find out the latest news, the trade started to die out in the mid-twentieth century due to the decline of the horse in transport and agriculture.

Blacksmith-forged iron cross in Old Abbey Graveyard, Fenagh Abbey, County Leitrim

HORSES

Before the age of tractors and cars, the horse was integral to Irish life, from agriculture to haulage and transport. In the west of Ireland, sure-footed donkeys were particularly suited to carrying loads across the rocky terrain, where horses would have struggled.

Horses and donkeys would carry loads of manure/seaweed, potatoes, turf and so on in creels (panniers, or *cliabh* in Irish), which were usually made from sally rods (willow, from the Latin *salix*), hazel rods and/or wood. A special type of creel, known as a *bardóg*, had a hinged bottom that could be opened by

This family is going to collect turf, with the boy riding the donkey and the girl sitting in the creel. Lough Melvin Road, Bundoran, County Donegal (© National Museums NI).

Horse ring on the wall of a church, Porterstown, County Dublin (built 1890). Horses would be tied to these while their owners went to mass.

pulling a stick to let the load fall onto the ground; this was particularly useful for manure. Creels hung on each side of the horse's back, so to balance the load it would be split into equal amounts on each side, but if there was only one item to transport (for example a firkin/small barrel of butter or even a child) stones would be used to balance it.

Our National Folklore Collection holds an account written in the 1930s, demonstrating how people engaged with horses and how important they were on a farm:

Turf slide-car with straw-harnessed pony outside a thatched house, Glendun, County Antrim. This type of cart was widely used in the eighteenth century. In later years, its use continued on in the mountainous regions of Ulster. (© National Museums NI.)

Of all the farmyard animals the farmer thinks most highly of the horse. It ranks next to the dog for intelligence and is the most valuable, as a general run, of all on the premises.

On the small farm one horse only is kept and so to get the work done two neighbouring farmers work together, this is called 'joined in the plough'. The two men work together in the fields throughout the year.

Each horse or mare has its own name as: Tommy, Daisy, Kate etc. When calling horses the sound 'plush,

plush' is made. When wanting them to go to the right side, 'Hoff, Hoff' and to the left 'Come Here, Come Here'. When calling a foal, Foalie, Foalie, is the usual call.

The horse's house is called the stable. The tying is called a halter which is placed on the animal's head, the rope on the halter is called the stock. This stock is passed through a ring and fastened to a block of wood which allows the animal to move its head at its ease but which at same time keeps it securely fastened.

Horse bridle, 1935 (© National Folklore Collection, UCD)

Mounting stone at a public house, which had accommodation and livery stables in the nineteenth century. Dunboyne, County Meath.

A colt is broken in when only eighteen or nineteen months. This is done gradually. First it is taught to lead. A halter is put on its head and it is led along by a rope. Next the colt is in to plough or mow with another steadier horse. Lastly when tired of this work it is made draw the cart.

Before commercial coir rope was introduced, rope, known as *súgán*, was made by twisting straw and it was used for making horse tack. Hay was used instead of straw when stronger but softer ropes were needed, such as parts of the harness where straw ropes would chafe or break.

Mounting stone (on the right) outside a building which, over the years, operated as a post office (as marked on nineteenth-century maps) and public house. The upright stone pillar (on the left), which horses would be hitched to, was the inspiration for the pub's most recent name, The Hitching Post. It operated here in the early twenty-first century. Ballycogley, County Wexford.

Wooden paving, Trinity College Dublin. Situated on what was the roadway under the front entrance arch, the wood deadened the sound of horses' hooves and cartwheels. The jostle stone (or bollard or base-protector) protected the building from damage from horses and carts.

When people went to mass, shops or fairs, they would tie their horses or donkeys to horse rings, which are still found on walls in villages and churches. Mounting stones, used to help people mount their horse or get into a cart, can still be seen at some buildings that had stables attached, such as coach houses or public houses.

There were so many horses that the streets were filthy with horse dung. In fact, there was so much readily available that piles of dung were used to halt a huge fire that swept through the Liberties area of Dublin in 1875. A million litres of whiskey had spilled from warehouse barrels and was flowing, on fire, down the streets. All efforts to douse it failed. Then the fire chief ordered that horse dung mounds be built, which dammed it and extinguished the fire.

Wheel-tracks, Phibsborough, Dublin

We can still see many remnants of our historical relationship with horses on our streets. In Trinity College Dublin, the original wooden block paving still lies under the entrance arch. In the nineteenth and early twentieth centuries, wooden block paving was common on our roads and in European and American cities. It offered better grip for horses' hooves and cartwheels, and absorbed the deafening clatter of the wheels' metal rims. They were commonly situated in carriage entrances to dampen the noise near the building. Bicycle rides were smoother over wooden paving too, although it could be slippery when wet. Wooden paving was also smelly and a public health officer in London launched an investigation to determine if it was the cause of eye inflammation and throat problems. While he could neither prove nor disprove the theory, he did find that the paving blocks were saturated with ammonia, broken down from horses' urine.

Most sett and cobblestone streets were later buried beneath asphalt, so surviving examples of wheel-tracks are rare. Wheel-tracks eased the burden

Horse trough, St Stephen's Green, Dublin

Tow-rope marks (the horizontal lines) on Granard Bridge (c.1810), Royal Canal, Dublin

on horses travelling up inclines, as cart or carriage wheels rolled more smoothly over them.

Horse troughs, providing water for thirsty horses, were often located at fountains or wells. A hole high up at one end lets water escape as it rises, to limit overflowing.

The industrial history of Irish canals is imprinted on its bridges, where we can still see the marks left by the friction of over a century of tow-ropes, as the horses towing barges passed by the bend. The ropes could pick up grit on the journey which, combined with the wet, increased their abrasiveness.

BRIDGES

Narrow stone bridges, only as wide as a person, can be found dotted around our landscape. Known as clapper bridges, some could date as far back as the thirteenth century, built as part of Christian abbey complexes to enable the monks to bring their grain to be ground at their mill. Some were built as recently as the mid-nineteenth century.

The name clapper may originate from the Latin *claperius*, which means a pile of stones. Flat slabs of stone of various sizes, some over two metres long and weighing up to a tonne, were laid across upright stones or piers. They may appear simple, but clapper bridges that cross wider stretches of water in particular demonstrate the ingenuity of their builders. They are curved horizontally based on the principle of the arch, so the stones are pushed tighter by the force of the water, thus strengthening the bridge. In some cases,

Clapper bridge in Graiguenamanagh, County Kilkenny, which linked the thirteenth-century Duiske Abbey with its mill. There is also a holy well visible at the top left.

Clapper bridge, known locally as the Stepping Stones, Ballingeary, County Cork. This bridge has a little island (on the left) to prevent erosion of the bridge by softening the force of the water as it meets the bridge.

The Stepping Stones, Newcastle, County Down, an earlier form of river crossing that later evolved into bridges (© National Library of Ireland)

Clapper Bridge, known locally as Ros a'Locha Stepping Stones, County Cork, was the first bridge erected across this river (Abha na Sróine)

This donkey is carrying panniers (creels) filled with turf, Dún Chaoin, County Kerry (© National Folklore Collection, UCD)

little islands were built alongside to prevent the bridge being eroded by the water.

While clapper bridges were invaluable to the local community, enabling people to cross rivers safely, with their donkeys and carts crossing alongside in the water, their humble nature meant that there aren't records of them before nineteenth-century maps, where they are denoted as a foot stick or foot bridge. Locals often call them stepping stones, likely a tradition that has carried down through the years from when they replaced earlier stepping stones. These could be quite restrictive; for example, people wanting to cross the stepping stones (predating the early nineteenth-century stone road bridge) linking Foaty Island (now Fota Island) to the mainland could not cross at high tide and had to wait for low tide for their horses to be able to cross safely.

A packhorse on a wooden bridge. The Pictorial Times, *1847.*

A bridge just wide enough to fit a packhorse, An Gharmain (Garroman), County Galway

Bunlahinch clapper bridge, County Mayo, the longest clapper bridge in Ireland at about 50 metres long. Estimates of its age vary, but it has been linked to a nineteenth-century initiative to create access between a church, school and cottages for converts to the Society for the Protection of Rights of Conscience, a short-lived venture of which only ruins remain. Note the openings in the parapet wall, which allow the water through when the river level is high.

Another early type of bridge that could be used for walking animals over without entering the water was the packhorse bridge. A packhorse is a horse or donkey used to carry loads across its back, so these bridges were the width needed to fit a horse or donkey loaded with panniers. They traditionally had low or no sides for the same reason.

THE POUND

Many towns and villages across Ireland hold the remnants of pounds, once enclosures for holding animals. Some have now been converted into village parks, but their tranquillity belies their chaotic and sometimes violent past.

From at least the fourteenth century, there was a system to impound animals, which developed over the centuries into a set of legal rules that applied to public pounds and manor pounds (owned by the lord of a grand estate). The enclosure into private ownership of lands that had been used for centuries as commonages to graze animals contributed to the accusations of trespass as people continued their traditions.

If an animal was straying and trespassing on land, the occupier of the land could organise for it to be seized. This could be ruthless – even two-week-old lambs that were still suckling were separated from their mothers to be taken to the pound after they jumped onto the walls of an estate in County Mayo.

If the animal's owner could be identified, for example through letters painted on it or the shape of an ear cut (denoting ownership), the occupier should approach them and request a payment called 'trespass'. If they refused to pay this, or if the owner was not identified, the animals could legally be impounded. A punishment was levied against the person impounding the animals if it could be proved that the owner was in fact known, and many cases came before local courts, with the owners saying they hadn't been approached to control their animals or their offer of recompense had been ignored.

The pound in Croghan, County Roscommon, with a stream running through the site. Pounds were built near sources of fresh water, as a supply was needed for the animals and for cleaning.

Once impounded, the pound-keeper would not release the animals until the appropriate payments were made. The fee was calculated in two parts. The first portion was the pound fee, paid to the pound-keeper, which was calculated according to the type of animal and the duration it was kept. For example, in 1871 the pound fee was 6d (sixpence) for a horse or cow for the first 72 hours, then 3d for each 72 hours thereafter, with an additional amount added on for the animal's sustenance. In addition, 'trespass' was due to the occupier of the trespassed land, with different rates for each animal type: in the same period, 2d for a sheep, 6d for a horse or cow, and 3s (three shillings) for a goat. These rates doubled if the land they had been found trespassing on was fattening pasture or planted with crops.

A notice would be posted in the police station about animals found, and unclaimed animals would be sold, with the proceeds going to the county. Sometimes animal owners would break into the pound to steal the animal back without paying the fees.

The pound-keeper, a respectable role, had to be appointed by the local justices. However, there were sometimes accusations of corruption. Some

Sign pointing to Pound Field, Kilskyre, County Meath

The pound in Castledermot, County Kildare, now a tranquil park

pound-keepers might hold a second job, as a bailiff or a herder employed by a landowner, for example. One local priest wrote about such a situation he was helping with: 'the bailiff and pound-keeper – two characters that should never be found in one person, the temptation to illegal pounding is so great'.

This conflict of interest was also found in a court case heard in Partry in County Mayo, where the pound-keeper, Mr Crystal, was employed by Lord Plunkett, the local landlord, who regularly impounded vast numbers of livestock found on his part of the mountain. The local pound was regularly crowded with as many as eighty sheep, leading to allegations of deterioration in the condition of the animals. On one occasion in 1860, the animal owners' solicitor described the 'continued annoyances and losses to which these poor people in Partree were subjected by the constant impounding of their cattle and sheep. At every hand's turn, and upon every wretched pretext, the animals were snapped at and sent to the pound, which was frequently choke full.' Since there were no fences on the land, the animals could wander anywhere, but instead of driving the animals back onto their owners' land, they were driven off to the pound by Lord Plunkett's staff.

Pound Lane, named after the local pound that was on this lane. Borris, County Carlow.

Numerous contentious cases came before the courts for a multitude of reasons related to pounds. In 1838, in Gloun in County Cork, the threat to bring a neighbour's goats to the pound for trespass money led to a struggle and a subsequent manslaughter charge. In another case in Kerry in 1891, the goats belonging to a man who had been evicted by an absentee English landlord strayed back to the land they were accustomed to graze on and were impounded, leading to a fine.

Whole mountains were swept clear of trespassing cattle. In 1892 in Castlewaller, County Tipperary, on several occasions a hundred cattle were impounded simultaneously. Similarly, in 1842, a constabulary force of fifty men were deployed to White Mountain in County Wexford while Charles Doyne and 'a strong party of his men' worked to impound all cattle committing trespass on the mountain. Immense crowds – reportedly thousands of people – gathered to oppose this violently, with 'threats that they would die before they would permit the cattle to be impounded'.

Sometimes there were legal cases for damages because pregnant animals gave birth in the pound, with the baby or even the adult animal subsequently dying.

Other social problems are also evident in the records. One incident, reported in 1835, involved the rector of Donegore in County Antrim. The owner of the land he was passing through on a hunt impounded his horse, saying that since the rector compelled him to pay tithes to the Church, the rector should pay him trespass. Tithes were a type of tax assessed at 10 per cent of the produce of an occupier's agricultural land (payable by people of all denominations to the Church of Ireland, an Anglican [Protestant] denomination). If the tithe was not paid, animals could be 'impounded for tithe', and then put up for auction to pay the debt.

The pound in Maynooth, County Kildare, situated on Pound Lane, with the river alongside

Three women with baskets (creels) gathering seaweed on the Irish coast. (© National Library of Ireland.)

THE SEA

FISHING

Fishing has been integral to life on the coast of Ireland since ancient times, providing a crucial source of food and trade. Archaeological evidence includes 7,000-year-old conical fish traps made from wooden rods, and widespread household refuse heaps, called middens, which include discarded shells. People would use bones as hooks, plant fibre for fishing lines, and they would hollow out logs to make boats (a 4,000-year-old log boat was found in an Irish bog). Later, people began to build fishery weirs and weave nets.

A traditional method of net fishing was seine fishing (from Old English *segne*, meaning dragnet), of which there is a record in Ireland as far back as

Fish curing in the late nineteenth/early twentieth century, Ardglass, County Down. Crews of women, including women from Scotland, migrated to various harbours, following where the herring was being fished. (© National Library of Ireland.)

During the operation of a fish palace here in the seventeenth century, press beams were slotted into these holes to weigh down the pilchards and press out the valuable train oil. Baltimore, County Cork.

1616. This could be done by day or by night (when the fish could be identified by the phosphorescence they caused in the water). Two rowing boats worked together, with the larger seine boat in the lead carrying the net. A lookout, who remained on land, shouted '*barriasc*' when he spotted the fish, and directed the boats towards the shoal with hand signals. The glow from the fish could be acres in size and the fishermen would know by its colour if the fish were mackerel or another species. The captain gave directions, in Irish – even after English became the everyday language of the people. The men in the lead boat strained hard to row it at high speed to complete a circle, with the smaller boat holding the other end of the net. Eventually both ends would be drawn together, completely enclosing the fish in a purse-like net. The masses of fish were then transferred on to the boat, basket by basket. The weight of the net when wet and its pressure when filled could drag the boats dangerously and caused multiple drowning tragedies.

In the seventeenth century, pilchards, an oily fish, were caught in this way. Preserving the fish was crucial since fresh fish could not be transported long distances. They would be cured with salt in fish 'palaces' immediately after being landed. The pilchards were washed, sprinkled with salt and stacked, and after a few weeks they would be rinsed and layered into barrels with more salt. Each barrel was placed under a hole in a wall into which a wooden beam was slotted and lay horizontally over the barrel with a weight hanging at the other end. Using gravity, this weight pressed the oil out of the fish. The oil, called 'train oil', was a valuable commodity in its own right, used in the preparation of leather and as fuel for lamps (similar to whale oil).

The return of shoals of fish was irregular, with pilchards or herring not guaranteed to return each year. Between 1810 and 1822 there were no herring at the Connemara coastline near Renvyle, which local superstition attributed to a drowning tragedy in a storm in 1809. In 1862, severe storms and rough seas caused the volume of herring on the west coast to drop so low that the fishing

Drying fish on the roof, Inis Mór, Aran Islands, 1935. Cod and ling were abundant in the summer and preserved as a vital food source for the winter months when fishing was not possible in the rough seas. In some designs, as on the Blasket Islands, houses were built against an earthen bank, so it was possible to walk onto the roof at the back of the house. (© Trinity College Dublin.)

Treating a currach with a layer of tar ('tarring the currach') to waterproof the boat (© National Library of Ireland)

population was described in official papers as 'dying out; and boats are to be seen lying idle on the beach'. Therefore, with these long depressions, skills and fishing equipment would be lost. Another challenge was the price of salt, with the government imposing duties that made fish curing uneconomical for many years and made the price of fish unmanageably variable. There was also a lack of investment by the government in Irish fishing infrastructure, such as building harbours, in contrast with the investment they made in English and Scottish infrastructure (whose fishermen fished in Irish waters and sold the fish they caught to Ireland). Since fishermen could not depend on their income from fishing alone, they often also farmed a small parcel of land to supplement it. When fishing and farming requirements coincided, which they often did, this land was tended to by the woman of the house.

Coastal fishing was mainly carried out in the summer, when the seas were calmer and the fish returned. Fishing life was a community partnership, with

Tar marks on Inis Mór, Aran Islands, County Galway, a remnant of the local fishermen applying tar to waterproof their currachs. This is likely the spot that Liam O'Flaherty describes in his short story 'The Stone', where the old man 'saw the upturned coracles on the flags among the boulders on the shore, their tarred bottoms gleaming in the sunlight'.

fishermen sharing boats: several men would carry the currach upside down and launch it to sea, with all boats setting out at the same time. They never left without a bottle of holy water attached to the frame, believing it afforded protection at sea, and dipped their finger over the side to bless themselves with sea water. It was considered bad luck to learn how to swim; that meant you doubted the seaworthiness of your boat, and it would only prolong the struggle if you were swept overboard. Back at home, a live shellfish (such as a limpet) was placed in the four corners of the house to ensure safe and plentiful fishing.

A common boat type in the west of Ireland was the timber-framed currach, over which fishermen would stretch animal hide (or, in later years, canvas) and then apply a waterproof layer of tar. (Tar would be produced by slowly heating peat or pine whilst limiting oxygen.) The agility of currachs suited the Irish coastline. They could be landed on the shore in most conditions, and were light enough to be carried to be stored in a safe pen.

It is often asked how the people of an island could not survive on fish during the Great Hunger. There were many obstacles in place. From the 1830s, the British government had established coastguard stations in prominent locations along the Irish coastline to control access to the sea and the use of its resources. Severe penalties were incurred for breaching this control; for example, in 1847, the worst year of the Great Hunger, thirteen currachs, fishing equipment and that day's catch were confiscated by the coastguard off

Currach pens at Purteen Harbour, Dooagh, Achill Island, County Mayo. Currachs would be carried ashore and tied down over a stand made of stones in a sheltered position, which stored the boats safely against the winds in the west of Ireland.

the coast of Achill Island because they had not been registered under a British regulatory requirement. Fishing equipment was also relinquished at this time because it was sold or pawned to buy food.

Rights to fishing an area, called 'several fishery rights' (meaning exclusive rights), were usually owned by the landlord class, benefiting a few wealthy landowners at the expense of the general public. Local fishermen might not be permitted to fish for salmon in their local rivers and lakes; for example, in the nineteenth century in Ballynakill Harbour in Connemara, one local tradition reveals that no salmon fishing (other than by the licence holder) was allowed within one mile of the estuary of the Dawros River.

A kiln on Blacksod Pier, County Mayo, which held a barking pan, where cotton fishing nets were 'barked' (cured). A large cauldron of water, into which oakum or cutch (a tar-like preservative) had been placed, was heated over a peat fire. The nets were soaked regularly in this mixture to prolong their life, which also resulted in dyeing them a brown colour. This tough task required community effort, with the nets weighing up to a ton each when wet.

The Fisheries Watchtower, Galway City, built in 1853 as a draft-netting station (similar to seine netting, but with one boat working with a net attached to a point on the shore), and as a watchtower to look out for poachers.

From the early nineteenth century, the landlord class arranged for Scottish fishery men to build large fishing traps by driving wooden stakes into the riverbed to form a V-shape. These became known as Scotch weirs. The water would flow through the wide end (the mouth) and essentially funnel the fish into a conical net at the narrow end (the head). There had been earlier versions of stake weirs, called head weirs, but these did not target salmon specifically, only worked on one tide, and allowed fish to pass upstream. Scotch weirs, on the other hand, worked on both the ebb and flow tides and were capable of catching hundreds of fish at a time, mainly salmon, which were then preserved in ice and transported by train to wider markets. Fish stocks depleted, as the salmon could not swim upstream to spawn. Indeed, a parliamentary debate noted that even tiny sprats could not pass out of these tightly woven traps. Unlike fishing by boat, Scotch weirs were not restricted

Head weir, Waterford Harbour, County Waterford, at low tide. This weir was the property of the Faithlegg Estate. Weir poles – pine trees 25–40 feet in length – were driven into the silt. These weirs, continuously maintained and repaired, date back many centuries and were the precursors to Scotch weirs.

by bad weather. This impacted the fishermen's food and livelihood right up the rivers, due to the decline in the fish available, and the weir also restricted navigation along the river. Many Scotch weirs were built in the Waterford Estuary, with their bounty exported to British tables, leading to local rioting and multiple clandestine expeditions by the local fishermen along the River Suir and the estuary to cut down the weirs. One such expedition during the Great Hunger resulted in the flat-bottomed boats (known as cots) of the 'poor fishermen of New Ross' being confiscated by the authorities for three fishing seasons. This restricted access also led to poaching, which of course resulted in more punishment if caught.

SEAWEED

Seaweed is a precious resource in Ireland and over the centuries has earned crucial income for coastal communities. As far back as the twelfth century, seaweed was harvested and distributed to the poor (as mentioned in a poem from the time). It was useful for fertilising the land: in rocky areas with little soil, seaweed was mixed with sand, manure, ash and other organic materials to create a nutrient-rich soil in which crops were grown.

During the Great Hunger, the nutritional value of seaweed helped coastal people to survive, but a tragedy in County Mayo in 1849 was explicitly stated to have been provoked by the effects of hunger. A newspaper reported how 'a father, his two sons, and two daughters, with a relative, driven by hunger went

Gathering seaweed on the coast, County Clare. This illustration was printed in 1882, with accompanying text describing the people's poverty, and how dillisk and carrageen moss seaweeds were both eaten and prepared for sale.

Two kelp burners on the Aran Islands, c.1915. Photograph by A.W. Cutler, published in National Geographic.

Three women with baskets (creels) gathering seaweed on the Irish coast. Liam O'Flaherty, in his short story 'The Stone', describes women doing this work: 'He saw the cocks [stacks] of dried seaweed and patches of seamoss, being bleached white, spread out, gathered that morning by the village women'. (© National Library of Ireland.)

out on the rocks on the shore of Clare Island to collect seaweed for food when, melancholy to relate, a wave passed over them, and on its return carried these six poor creatures into the sea, and they were all drowned.'

From the seventeenth century, seaweed processing became an important industry along our coastlines. When processed, seaweed becomes kelp, a critical ingredient for producing soap and glass, bleaching linen, and producing iodine, used in medicine and photography.

There were strict rules around entitlement to seaweed. The villagers might appoint one or two men to control the process around the collection and distribution of seaweed to ensure fairness (as was done on Achill Island). The arrangements varied in different areas, but generally, once the seaweed was gathered from common areas, it was apportioned by lottery to people who held land. Those who did not own land were limited to the pickings from

Seaweed garden, Achill Island, County Mayo

the small section of beach allocated to paupers. Strips of the strand were also allocated to people (which might be based on their local landholding or rent paid), where they might construct seaweed gardens. These were large stones set in the sea on which seaweed grew, taking three years to reach maturity.

These arrangements could lead to discord, with numerous legal challenges in court. In 1888, a Kerry newspaper wrote about the right to cut seaweed: 'The question of individual title to the foreshore has frequently been raised by landlords in this country … but the general public were successful in defeating the attempted monopoly.' Discord could escalate to allegations of trespass, people forcibly carrying off seaweed, and even violence. In Ballylongford in County Kerry in 1845, a notice was posted on the door of the police barracks warning the constable that if he dared attempt 'to prevent the people from cutting seaweed at Carrig-island, to have his coffin prepared'.

Gathering seaweed, County Galway (© National Folklore Collection, UCD)

Kelp kiln, with kelp drying on walls, and kelp and carrageen moss stacks (thatched). Quilty, County Clare, 1935 (© National Folklore Collection, UCD).

Gathering seaweed, either by harvesting it from rocks or collecting the stems that had become dislodged by seasonal storms, was a community effort. An oral history of the Blasket Islands, off the coast of County Kerry, describes this activity: 'At daybreak, stripped of everything but my drawers, with a rake to gather the weed, out I'd go up to my neck in the sea.'

It was a dangerous task. A father and two young men, his sons, drowned while cutting seaweed on a rock in 1848 in Dunkelly West, County Cork, and the following year, five young men (including four brothers) and two young women drowned when their boat sank near Ballyshannon in County Donegal, despite jettisoning the seaweed over the side. Both incidents took place during the Great Hunger.

Once it was harvested, bundles of seaweed were floated on low tide to be collected by currachs on the rising tide, and when the bundles reached dry land, the seaweed was laid in piles for many days on walls or rocks to be air-dried.

Finally, the air-dried seaweed was burned slowly for up to twenty-four hours in a kiln from which visitors described white plumes of smoke rising all along the coastline, visible for miles. The kilns could be stonelined holes in

Kelp kiln, Cornarona, County Galway

Seaweed factory, dating to the late nineteenth century, Inis Mór, Aran Islands, County Galway

the ground or raised stone structures. The pervasive smell of the oily smoke drifted so far that villages fifteen miles away could tell when their neighbours were burning their seaweed. The seaweed had to be gradually added to the kiln and the work was arduous and filthy. The final product was a hard mass called kelp, which was broken into blocks and then sold. Later, seaweed processing became an industry in certain areas, with larger factories being built.

SALT

Remnants of saltworks, once busy industrial centres, lie in ruins along our coastline. People needed salt for many uses, including food preservation, attaching natural dyes to fabrics, and in the manufacture of pigments used in ancient monastic manuscripts. There is reference to making salt from brine in salt pans on the coast of County Down as early as the thirteenth century. These earliest methods of producing salt used only seawater, captured at high tide in a reservoir known as a bucket pot, which could be a natural rock pool or a hole quarried into the rock.

Eighteenth-century saltworks at Pans Rock (its name deriving from salt pans), Ballycastle, County Antrim, where the availability of local coal made saltworks viable. The steps lead to a naturally formed reservoir in the rock.

Aerial view of the cut-rock steps at Pans Rock leading to the natural rock reservoir, seen down at the waterline (front, left of centre)

When the tide receded, and the impurities in the water were allowed to settle to the bottom, the water was transferred at intervals to huge metal salt pans built over a firepit or kiln, sometimes making efficient use of the same fire as lime kilns. Specialist knowledge was needed to control the speed of evaporation to ensure the quality of taste and size of the crystals, with small-grained salt requiring higher temperatures. The damp salt was laid out to dry in the sun, near the fire, or hung in straw bags, and later transferred to purpose-built salt storehouses.

Top: Seventeenth-century saltworks at Slade Harbour, County Wexford, which used halite and seawater brine, rather than depending on seawater alone to make salt. Its pier-side location likely complemented the preservation of fish with salt.

Left: Tunnel under Pans Rock. One theory is that it was created by mining a coal seam, but a folklorist working for the National Folklore Collection recorded it as a kiln (fired by locally mined coal) under the natural rock, used to accelerate natural evaporation during operation of the salt pans.

Men working on an industrial salt pan, with salt on the cart, at Carrickfergus, County Antrim, near where rock salt was mined. A man using a 'skimmer' would rake the salt crystals to the side. The steam from these types of works could be seen for some distance, especially on cold winter days. The 'dirty salts' from the floor went to farmers to feed to cattle to supply essential minerals. (© National Museums NI.)

A later method, for which there is evidence from the seventeenth century (such as the operation at Slade Harbour, County Wexford), was to import rock salt (a mineral called halite, mined in Britain and later in Ireland). This was dissolved in local seawater to make a more concentrated brine. The water was then evaporated off, leaving the salt. The Irish salt industry went into decline after 1825 when salt duties were abolished, thus increasing competition from British salt.

Many placenames around the Irish coast evidence their salt-making heritage, such as Salthill (Galway and Dublin), Salt Island (Strangford Lough, County Down), Saltpans (County Donegal), and most likely Salterstown (County Louth) in association with monastic industry at Mellifont Abbey.

Saltworks building, Ray, County Donegal

The wider saltworks site at Ray, County Donegal

A community group gathered at harvest time (© National Library of Ireland)

THE LAND

CATTLE

Our earliest Irish stories tell of cattle raids between neighbouring kings and queens, sometimes with thousands being rustled at one time and involving legendary figures such as Cú Chulainn and Queen Medb (Maeve). The countryside of Ireland is dotted with over 40,000 ringforts (*lios*), the remnants of ancient farming enclosures. Some were built of stone but more often they were created by piling earth taken from a ditch (fosse) into a circular mound (bank). They were an early form of farm compound, and many are estimated to date from the fifth century AD, or earlier. They contained a house and farm buildings, and the main economic activity was raising cows for milk. Ringforts, commonly called fairy forts, are strongly associated with superstitions and belief in the fairies and so have often remained untouched through the years.

Cattle farming continued through the centuries. Even under British rule, cattle production grew in the sixteenth century, as animals could be moved quickly in the face of imminent threat, whereas static grain stores could be seized or destroyed. Cattle were valuable not just for their meat and milk, but also for their hides and skins, a commodity that was traded far and wide. However, in the seventeenth century, cattle were the subject of a series of British laws imposed to protect English farmers' profits, notably the Cattle Acts, which prohibited the import into England of Irish cattle and meat products.

Superstitions grew up around protecting cattle, the farm's most valuable asset. They would be herded into the smoke or embers of festival bonfires (the May bonfire or the midsummer bonfires on St John's Eve), or the ashes or embers of these fires might be placed (or marked in crosses using a charred stick) in the dairy to protect the milk and butter from evil magic.

Transhumance was practised from probably the eleventh century AD. Some members of a community would migrate, with their dairy cattle, to graze them in the hills (where no rent was due) rather than using their rented land, which could instead be used to grow hay or other crops. The practice was commonly known as booleying, from the Irish term *buaile*, which had various

Leacanabuaile stone ringfort, County Kerry, possibly ninth century. The name means 'hillside of the milking-place' and it is thought to have been built as a farming homestead, with its hilltop position providing a natural defence and clear visibility. Within their circular enclosure, ringforts typically contained roofed living spaces, and there is evidence of animal pens to shelter valuable livestock.

meanings, including 'milking place', 'milking place of summer pasturage' and 'small grazing field'. The practice followed a predictable pattern and the same site was used each year, either within the parish or in the adjoining hills. As the grazing became exhausted, the cattle would sometimes be moved on to another site, usually staying within a distance of 7.5 miles (12km) of the village. The opposite was the case in the Burren in County Clare, a unique limestone habitat, where the cattle were driven onto winterage pastures for winter grazing. When booleying during the summer, the herders, often the younger generation of women (chosen for their association with the household's dairy tasks), would usually stay in booley houses or huts for six months. Their daily tasks included milking the cattle morning and evening (keeping the milk fresh

Woman driving cattle, Achill Island, County Mayo (© National Library of Ireland)

Slievemore, Achill Island, County Mayo. These houses continued to be used as booley houses after the Great Hunger, when the village lay deserted. Note the lazy beds, which remain intact.

in a stream) and making butter, which they would bring to an agreed location once a week to be collected and brought back to the main home. They might bury it in the bog temporarily to keep it fresh, hence we find remains of bog butter. People remembered their time spent there with fondness; they enjoyed more social freedom away from the usual constraints of the village.

The practice declined from the early nineteenth century, for a combination of reasons. Some landlords claimed rights over the commonages used for booley pasture; imported Scottish sheep were grazed on the land; field ownership and divisions were restructured after the Great Hunger (home holdings became larger); and there were social changes, such as young people migrating to farms in other regions to provide summer labour for a cash wage.

However, placenames remind us of the land's past use: many placenames contain 'boley' (such as Boley Hill in County Wexford) or *'buaile'* (such as Buaile Beag or Booleybeg, County Galway), which may point to previous booleying activities there.

A village at Slievemore (now deserted) is a good example of how agricultural methods impacted people's living arrangements and the landscape. Before the Great Hunger, it was the largest village on Achill Island, containing 137 houses. These houses were built on either side of a linear roadway, with thatched roofs, now collapsed, and no windows, which kept the harsh island winds out. The majority of the houses were one-roomed cabins, where between eight and fifteen people lived per house, and at night their cattle slept in the house at the end of the room furthest from the fire, separated only by a channel.

Following the Great Hunger, this village gradually became deserted, with the lazy beds (potato ridges) remaining in pristine condition as the villagers never got to harvest their potato crop. Some of these houses were later, as recently as the early twentieth century, used as booley houses, where people would come during the summer months to mind their cattle and graze them on the mountain. Achill Island is thought to be one of the last places in Ireland to have practised this lifestyle.

RUNDALE

Closely associated with booleying and seaweed entitlement was the farming system called rundale, a community system particularly suited to mixed-quality landscapes. Records of the practice date it to at least the sixteenth century. People did not know it by this name at the time: it was just their way of life in the areas where it was practised.

In modern times we are used to fields being joined together as part of a single farm, but under rundale the community leased land from the landlord as joint tenants. Within the area, people lived in a cluster of houses called a clachan (*clochán*). Each family was allocated multiple scattered pockets of land according to the rent they paid. The aim was that each tenant would

Slievemore, Achill Island, County Mayo. The rundale system operated in the fields shown in the distance, with the divisions by banks still visible.

get a fair portion of the best land by a river, and portions of the lesser-quality land (for example boggy or sandy soil). There might be one fence enclosing the arable land, called the 'infield', which was used for cultivating crops, with each family growing in their own pocket of land. Further away from the clachan, and outside the fence, was the less fertile 'outfield', which could be used for grazing cattle all year or for growing less intensive crops in suitable months. In winter, every family's livestock would be allowed into the infield to roam, improving it with their dung and the action of their hooves, so it was important that there was no permanent fencing dividing the infield; rather, delineations such as low earthen mounds or furrows would be used. In the spring and summer, the livestock would be moved away to the booleying

A community group gathered at harvest time (© National Library of Ireland)

pastures, allowing both the infield and the outfield to be cultivated (or for the hay growing in the outfield to mature).

The plots (depending on the agreement in an area) might be redistributed by lot at intervals (perhaps annually) to ensure fairness and spread risk, for example so that flooding would not happen to the same person two years running. A consequence of these changes was confusion and often disputes over boundaries.

This farming system relied on the community supporting each other, and many farming tasks were done on a *meitheal* system, meaning team or work party. Groups of neighbours would pool their efforts to cut turf (peat), thresh oats, reap the harvest, and collect and burn seaweed (see page 74). If somebody needed help on their land, they would gather a *meitheal* and people that helped for a day on their neighbour's farm expected a day's work on their own farm in return.

A *meitheal* could also be used in livestock farming; for example, on the Great Blasket Island there was communal sheep farming, where the men would gather all the sheep, clip each lamb's ear in the same pattern as its mother, shear and dip the sheep, and transport them to and from the mainland. It was a fair system built on co-operation and supportive group practices, and must have stretched back to ancient times, as there were rules under the old Gaelic legal system for when a plough was owned in partnership with neighbours. This indigenous legal system, called Brehon Law, operated prior to English rule, and was arbitrated by 'Brehons'. It was first written down in the seventh century AD and persisted until the seventeenth century, when it was replaced by English common law.

Transporting pigs, Inis Meáin, Aran Islands, County Galway, 1925. In many areas under rundale, each family would keep pigs, but the killing of the pigs would be staggered, with the meat shared out between the families so that every family had meat throughout the year. (© Trinity College Dublin.)

Many coastal communities had to supplement fishing incomes with farming, and when the men fished most of the farming work fell to the women. Women's work, which contributed enormously to a household's cash income, might include raising geese, hens, turkeys and bonhams (piglets) for sale, and women had to do a lot of physical labour: drawing water from the well, milking the cows, making butter, feeding the animals, and carrying heavy loads of turf and crops in a creel on their backs.

TRAVELLING LABOURERS

From the eighteenth century, due to poverty at home, men and women would move temporarily for months at a time from poor areas in the west to the richer lowlands (east Munster and south Leinster) or to Scotland, to help with the harvest. They were known as *spailpíní fánacha* – wandering or travelling

Irish harvesters on their way to England, 1881

An example of a hand plough, or loy (styles varied according to the soil of an area, as did their name: they were usually called a spade or loy). The dibbing tool on the right, called a steeveen, made a hole to plant seed potatoes. They are resting on an old settle bed. (On display at Glenview Folk Museum, Ballinamore, County Leitrim.)

labourers – and were a common sight migrating to their temporary jobs, carrying their spades or scythes and travelling the long distance on foot. One account described how they would walk from Kerry in their bare feet with their boots slung on leather laces over their shoulder, so as to save their boots for the stubble fields and for Sundays. Hiring fairs were held to select workers, with demand for spadesmen in spring (for tilling the fields) and for mowers in autumn (mowing the hay with a scythe). The journey could be dangerous; Kevin Danaher, the Irish folklore collector, tells how twenty-seven poor harvesters who were waiting for their ship at the Pigeon House in Dublin Harbour in 1790 were taken by a press gang and forced to join the British navy.

The plough was used where available and where the land permitted, but soil was mostly tilled by hand with a spade or loy. This was a handheld tool with a step (or two steps) used to drive the blade powerfully into the soil, which would then be turned to a depth of about a foot. Since Irish labour was so cheap, it was even common for multiple labourers with spades to be hired on larger farms, even though the land was suitable for the use of a plough. In fact, hand digging resulted in a better crop. The spade they used should measure to its user's shoulders and its length became an actual unit of measurement, usually taken to be five and a half feet long including its handle. Field sizes could be agreed by marking out the ground with the spade as a measuring stick to determine, for example, 800 spades long.

The poverty at home for the landless class necessitated the migration to do this work, as they needed the money to pay for the extortionate rents due in November each year. The potential to earn even small sums of money sent people to work abroad. When the workers returned home, these were occasions of elation and celebration: however, not everybody returned home safely. In summer 1894, thirty-two migratory workers were drowned when a boat transporting eighty to one hundred people from Achill Island capsized in Clew Bay, County Mayo. They had been travelling to Scotland to pick potatoes, with the income needed to repay loans that had been advanced to their families to buy seed potatoes (as their own had been destroyed by blight the year before). The twenty-five girls and young women would have

The mass grave of the thirty-two victims of the Clew Bay tragedy, who drowned in 1894 on their way to Scotland to pick potatoes. Kildownet, Achill Island, County Mayo.

brought home no more than ten pounds each for this endeavour, and the seven men between twelve and fifteen pounds each. Among the dead were multiple members of the same families, including three young sisters. They were usually the main breadwinners of their families (including Mrs Doogan, a mother of two young children, whose husband was going blind). Similarly, in 1937, ten boys aged thirteen to twenty-three died (again away doing migratory work picking potatoes in Scotland) when they, and sixteen others who survived, were locked for the night in a cabin that caught fire.

Then a more permanent migration to America became typical, and most of those who left never returned. In his unpublished memoir recording his reminiscences of West Breffni in County Leitrim, Anthony Mulvey tells how passage money was sent home by relations who had previously emigrated and the children in school talked about the day they would follow their sisters or brothers. He goes on to describe how, in the 1880s and 1890s, as many as ten young people would depart from one area on the same morning, having been blessed by the local priest at the previous Sunday's mass. Each family would hold a traditional event the night before departure; the 'American wake', a mixture of party and pain. The next morning, the migrant would be accompanied part of the way on their journey by the attendees of the party, led by a flute player, and converge with other similar processions of other migrants coming from all directions, after which heartbreaking scenes of separation followed. Scenes like this played out all over the country; in Wexford, a location at a river crossing became known as *Geata Na nDeor* or Gate of Tears, the last place where people leaving Clonegal parish to emigrate could look back and see their native valley and hills.

As Mulvey's notes in his memoir, 'Thus, lives that might, under proper national and social conditions, be devoted to the upbuilding of their own land, went to make another land great'. There they slept 'their last long sleep in American soil'.

RELIANCE ON POTATOES

On the eve of the Great Hunger, Asenath Nicholson, an American visitor who travelled around Ireland, encountered an old woman struggling to carry a sack of potatoes on her back in County Tipperary. She later wrote, 'But in every place I go, woman is made a beast of burden; and where this is allowed, and men are not paid for their toil, no legislation can elevate a people.'

The Irish people had suffered great poverty under British rule. Large estates had come to be owned by a relatively small number of landlords (many absentee, living in Britain) and the land rented to tenants through various methods, all resulting in poor legal rights where rent could be increased if the tenant made any improvements to the house or the land, while the tenant could be evicted at any time and for any reason. This treatment of the Irish was also noted by Nicholson: 'If the poor tenant improves the premises, he must be turned out or pay more. If he do not improve it, he is a lazy dirty Irishman, and must be put out for that.'

At this time, Catholic land ownership was in the single digits, and around 40 per cent of landholdings measured less than ten acres. Another group not counted in that figure, landless labourers, accounted for about 40 per cent of the population in 1845. They depended on an arrangement known as conacre, where they rented small plots of land for just one season and might 'pay' their rent by supplying their labour to the landlord's farm.

Among wider impacts, a series of oppressive Penal Laws enacted in Ireland by the British government from the seventeenth century systematically

Lazy beds (potato ridges) on the coast, Achill Island, County Mayo

excluded Catholics (who made up the majority of the Irish population) from land ownership, aiming to diminish their economic power and reducing them to a subservient position. They were forbidden to purchase land or inherit a full farm – on the death of the father the land had to be broken up between all his male children, and this, compounded by rapid population growth in the preceding century, ultimately resulted in generational shrinking of farms to unsustainable sizes.

Another drain on the resources of occupiers of land over one acre were tithes, payments due (even from Catholics) to maintain the Protestant established state Church. Tithes were a type of tax (payable in cash) assessed

The characteristic stripes of old lazy beds on small plot divisions can be seen high on this mountain in Connemara, County Galway

Men storing potatoes in a pit, Newcastle, County Down (© National Museums NI)

at the value of 10 per cent of the produce of an occupier's agricultural land. Failure to pay meant authorities could seize your produce or goods. Any grain people grew, or other farm produce, would have to be sold to get the cash to pay these bills. Similarly, the income from these marketable crops could be used to pay land rents.

In areas with small landholdings, and in such constrained financial conditions, the only viable crop that enabled people to feed their large families was the potato, which produced a higher yield and provided more calories per acre than other crops and was highly nutritious, almost a complete diet in itself. It became a mainstay of people's diet: men ate around 14 pounds of potatoes (6.4kg) and women 11 pounds (5kg) per day, split across equal meals. Potatoes thrived in the Irish climate and could be grown in the poorest of soils, when improved with lime (see page 101), seaweed (page 69) or burnt peat, and grew successfully even on rocky mountainsides.

The method used to grow potatoes was in 'lazy beds', where ridges were created by turning the earth with a loy (spade) inwards from each side to form a long ridge in the middle. The area from which the soil came was called the furrow and was approximately the same width as the ridge. The seed potatoes were then planted on the ridge and covered over with more soil, and later, more earth would be piled up around them from the furrow again and again as the stalks grew higher. Eventually, the ridge would become quite high.

At the May and midsummer festivals, bonfires would be lit. The smoke blowing over the crops, or ashes from the fire applied to the corners of the field (or a coal thrown into the field), was believed to protect the potatoes from blight.

Once harvested, the usual method of storing the potatoes was to pile them into pyramidal heaps in pits dug into the soil, then cover them with dry rushes laid upright and about six inches of clay to keep them dry and protect them from rats and frost.

This heavy reliance on one crop made the majority of Irish people's diet incredibly vulnerable, and in 1845, the potato crop succumbed to a blight, with diseased potato tubers rotting under the ground, as described by a land agent turned property owner, William Steuart Trench about Cardtown, County Laois, in his memoir written years later:

> The leaves of the potatoes on many fields I passed were quite withered, and a strange stench, such as I had never smelt before, but which became a well-known feature in 'the blight' for years after, filled the atmosphere adjoining each field of potatoes ... The crop of all crops, on which they depended for food, had suddenly melted away.

Remains of potato lazy beds still lie all over Ireland, untouched perhaps since their potatoes rotted under the earth.

LIME

In the years leading up to the Great Hunger, the English writer William Makepeace Thackeray travelled through Ireland and described how in 'the mountains at night, the kilns may be seen lighted up in the lonely places, and flaring red in the darkness'.

The kilns in question were masonry ovens for burning stone to create a whitish substance called lime, which had multiple uses. It was used to improve soil and reduce the acidity of peat soil, and was scattered over the ridges of lazy beds to kill cutworms (a pest that attacks the potato crop by 'cutting' the stalks at the soil line). Lime was used in the tanning industry to remove hair from animal hides and in the linen industry in the bleaching process. It could also be sprinkled into a well to kill insects and its odour-neutralising properties meant it was recommended for use in workhouse burials during the Great Hunger.

Lime kiln (front right) at Timogue, County Laois, amidst the ruins of other agricultural buildings. Lime kilns were often an integral part of farming infrastructure.

Whitewashed thatched cottage, possibly in County Kerry. (Photograph by J.M. Synge © Trinity College Dublin.)

When further processed, lime formed the active ingredient in making a versatile, breathable mortar for plastering walls and setting masonry. When mixed with water to a thin consistency, it made whitewash for coating walls, which formed a durable barrier from the weather and gave the houses their traditional appearance. When used inside, its whiteness reflected light to brighten small, dark rooms, and it had properties that killed fleas, bacteria and mould. Fresh cow manure would be diluted and strained, and then painted onto the wall and left for a few days to dry. When whitewashed over, it was snow white, and prevented smoke coming through the whitewash. But whitewashing would not be done in May, as it was believed to be bad luck ('If you whitewash in May you sweep the luck away').

In the eighteenth and early nineteenth centuries it became common for Irish farms to have their own lime kiln in areas where there was plentiful limestone, or farmers grouped together to build a communal kiln. While

Lime kiln at Lavistown, County Kilkenny. Lime kilns were built against a bank for ease in carting the stone to the top.

*Two boys standing at the edge of a smoking lime kiln pit, Loch Conaortha, County Galway.
(Photograph by Caoimhín Ó Danachair © National Folklore Collection, UCD.)*

there were variations in kiln types, the most common were rectangular stone buildings built against an earthen bank, with a shaft up through the centre (made of sandstone or brick to withstand the heat) that remained open at the top. The limestone, usually from a quarry, was broken to 'about the size of a goose egg' and carted up to this hole via the earthen bank, along with fuel: turf (peat), culm (balls of compressed yellow clay and coal dust) and/or furze (whins or gorse, which crackled as it burned due to its high oil content).

The kiln was then packed with alternating layers of limestone and fuel, and the top of the kiln was 'walked' by the men to pack it. They then lit the fire from a hole at the bottom called the 'eye', which acted as a vent to draw in air for the fire. This was also where the lime was raked out twice a day, once the

Hole at the top of a lime kiln, Hook Head, County Wexford

fire had burned gradually up through the layers. As the load dropped down, more was loaded from the top and so it could be burning for weeks or months, spewing its clouds of smelly bluish smoke.

Lime burning was a skilled job, since the correct temperature and gas flow through the kiln had to be constantly maintained, and it was a dangerous one,

Lime kiln at Cullohill, County Laois, with the shape of the circular hole on top still visible

with numerous incidents of burning injuries or agonising death. The men had to stand on the top of the contents to break up the stone as it burned, and it often sank, trapping them up to the waist in the burning fuel and hot stone. A crust would form at the top, which misleadingly looked as if the fire had gone out, when in fact it continued to burn underneath at temperatures above 900°C. Often a fellow worker trying to help their trapped companion would also fall victim to the fire. Due to the unguarded hole at the top and the need to run the kiln through the night in darkness, fall injuries were also common, with workers falling in and the smooth internal walls offering no grip to climb out. The flaring red ovens attracted members of the public to their warmth on cold, dark nights, and tramps would gather there, perhaps roasting stolen ducks or geese in the heat from the kiln. A more sinister event was recorded by Thackeray when he was shown a lime kiln in 1842 and told that the guard of a mail coach had been seized and roasted alive in it.

Some people were overcome by fumes and many fell into the open hole, including a homeless man in 1873 who was never identified, as his 'face was almost burned to a cinder'. In Midleton, County Cork, in 1833, five people died in a lime kiln, having been overcome by fumes. A worker descended into the kiln to remove some stones, but when he didn't return, another man followed to investigate, and then a third man. When none returned, the wives of two of the men followed in turn. Finally, another two men were lowered with ropes and almost suffocated, but were hauled up and saved. The five lifeless bodies were found on the surface of the limestone within the kiln.

In happier scenes, a marriage tradition associated with lime kilns usually took place at Halloween. Women would throw a ball of yarn from the top of the kiln and the man who twisted it up would be their future husband.

Increased cost of fuel, better transport (via railways) and improved kiln design saw production of lime mostly moving to more efficient industrial kilns in the second half of the nineteenth century. Large quantities of lime were needed to feed the construction associated with the Industrial Revolution, making local lime kilns much less relevant, and so the landscape is now dotted with their abandoned ruins.

MILLING

Milling was an important daily activity throughout Ireland from prehistoric times. Nuts, dried wheat, corn and other grains were crushed to make flour for food. Hazelnuts and grain dating to c.3500 BC have been found at Tuckmill Hill in County Wicklow. Grinding stones have been found across the country, including prehistoric saddle querns whose loose hand-stone (called a rubber) was worked backwards and forwards (rubbing rather than rolling) across a larger saddle-shaped stone to grind the grain.

Also from prehistoric times, it is thought by some experts that the rounded depressions in many bullaun stones (sacred stones believed by some to hold curative properties; see page 166) may have been made by ancient people grinding, rather like a pestle and mortar today and similar to grindstone depressions made by indigenous people in America.

Innovation progressed to the invention of rotary querns, which continued to be used up to recent centuries. These had an upper circular stone (called the runner) lying horizontally on a second circular stone (the stationary bed-

Saddle quern and rubber, 3800–2700 BC, found at White Park Bay, County Antrim (© National Museum of Ireland)

Ancient bullaun stone, Gortavoher, County Tipperary. Prehistoric grinding is one theory for the indentations found in these stones. Perhaps a woman would sit at each depression grinding corn with a loose stone (similar to the stones now known as the Petrified Dairy on pages 167–169). This stone then became a sacred stone, believed to hold the imprints of a saint's knees and to be a cure for warts. The stone was moved by a farmer over a century ago and mysteriously reappeared back in its correct position.

Rotary quern, Cill Buaine, County Kerry. Hand milling was deemed a woman's job. If two women were operating a rotary quern, they would push the wooden handle to each other, creating a rotary action, and with their spare hand each would feed the grain into the hole, called the eye. (© National Folklore Collection, UCD.)

stone), the weight of the stone making grinding more efficient. The runner stone was rotated via a handle (usually made of wood) inserted into a hole at one side. The grain was fed into the central hole as the quern stone turned, and milled flour came out from the sides.

People were not always allowed to use their querns freely. Under a feudal custom introduced by the Anglo-Normans known as 'suit to the mill', with examples still applying well into the eighteenth century, tenants were legally compelled to bring their cereals to the lord's mill to be ground, with a toll (a proportion of the flour ground) payable to the lord's miller. There is a record of the eighteenth-century proprietor of Kesh Mill in County Fermanagh organising for local querns to be destroyed so that business would channel through his own mill, but one quern did survive, thus creating secretive milling activity in the area: 'when any neighbour would borrow the quern, it was as carefully concealed from [the miller], as an illicit still would now be hidden from an exciseman'.

A similar functionality applies to how millstones work in purpose-built mills. Water-powered mills were in use in Ireland from around the seventh century AD, as evidenced in early Irish manuscripts and by scientifically dated timbers. This is the earliest evidence of the craft of millwrighting (mill erecting) in Europe, and under an eighth-century law the millwright (*saer muilinn*) was accorded minor noble status. In these operations, larger millstones usually lay horizontally, one on top of the other. They were rotated by the power generated by the water (or wind). The flow of water was controlled via a man-made channel called a mill race (also protected under the ancient laws).

Rotary querns and millstone, uncertain date. (On display at Glenview Folk Museum, Ballinamore, County Leitrim.)

Millstones at St Moling's Ecclesiastical Village, County Carlow, recovered from the river bed at the end of the nineteenth century. Local tradition holds that these are the millstones of the saint's seventh-century mill.

There are remnants of millstone production along our coasts. Sandstone was particularly in demand as it was the best stone for grinding, but it did result in fine grit entering the flour, which, when consumed, wore down tooth surfaces, evidenced by the worn teeth found in skeletal remains. At these coastal millstone quarries, there was a special method of quarrying the large blocks of stone to keep them in one piece, using the natural resource of the sea. The men chiselled out a rough disc shape from the cliff, leaving the base attached to the rock, and would then hammer wooden wedges into hollows. The wood would swell when the incoming tide covered them and split the millstone away from the base rock. We can still see from the abandonment of partially formed millstones the heartbreaking evidence that a flaw must have eventually been found in the stone after days, if not weeks, of labour.

There is also evidence of probable transportation mishaps where fully formed millstones still lie by the waterside; it is thought they fell and were damaged and so were abandoned.

A mill race, an artificial water channel for controlling the flow of water to a mill. Graiguenamanagh, County Kilkenny.

Top: Fully formed millstones, of a rare sandstone particularly suited to millstones, lying on a quarry's pier on the Hook peninsula, County Wexford. The finished millstone would be strapped onto the underside of a boat, which would float it up with the rising tide.

Left: Millstone quarry, with several abandoned attempts to extract millstones.

Broken or worn millstones can be found all over the country, having been discarded after their initial use was exhausted, to be reused as boundary markers, cartwheel binding stones (see page 34) and gravestones.

Supernatural powers were associated with millstones. It was believed that you could invoke a curse by turning the millstone in the opposite direction to normal. In the Kiltimagh area in County Mayo, a cruel landlord called Burke was cursed in this way by members of local families gathered at the mill. That same night, the landlord died and all his near relations met with sudden death soon after, with one drowning in a canal and another killed in a quarrel.

Another mystical story associated with millstones involves St Ciarán of Saigir who, having been condemned to death in the fifth century AD, was said to have been chained to a millstone and rolled off a cliff into the sea. He miraculously floated to Cornwall in England, to become their patron saint, known as St Piran (according to some beliefs).

Many placenames across Ireland derive from the local mill, such as Mill Street, Millrace Road and Milltown.

IRON

Lying on top of our harvested bogs are exposed areas of rust-coloured bog iron ore. Not far underneath, lumps of bog iron ore could be located by prodding the soft ground with sticks until a thud was felt. This iron had formed near the surface through the bacterial reaction between iron-rich groundwater and oxygen. As the Irish historical author and topographer Charles Smith wrote in 1756, 'Most of the bogs, and many of the mountains, abound with this ore.'

Bog iron ore shining bright orange on top of a bog near Banagher, County Offaly

A recreation of an ancient bloomery furnace using clay formed into brick shapes. The wooden section will be removed to make the opening.

Over two thousand years ago, ancient people discovered that by smelting iron ore at high temperatures, they could transform it into usable iron metal. One method was to mould earth into clay 'bricks', which they used to construct a small chimney shaft over a shallow pit, into which they layered the iron ore with charcoal. In temperatures that would reach around 800°C, the oxygen would be stripped away, leaving a semi-solid spongey mass of pure iron 'bloom', which is why we now call these bloomery furnaces. The bloom was then hammered while still molten to purify it and create an ingot of iron, which was later forged into metal objects such as knives and swords.

A recreation of an ancient bloomery furnace at Banagher Furnace Festival, County Offaly. The clay 'door' is drying on the top of the furnace before being used to seal up the opening.

This transformative quality, turning raw ore into powerful iron weapons, would have seemed like alchemy to our ancient ancestors, so this may be where the age-old belief in the supernatural qualities of iron comes from. Irish people believed iron repelled malevolent entities such as the *sidhe* (fairies) who live in the otherworld, and they held blacksmiths, who could manipulate this iron, in high regard.

The technology of these small furnaces progressed to a greater scale and large stone structures called blast furnaces were constructed from at least the sixteenth century. They were sited near iron ore quarries, although transporting the ore could take great manual effort. There is a local tradition attached to the furnace in Druminalass, County Leitrim that 'barefooted local men carried the iron ore in creels on their backs down the mountain side to the lake, a distance of 5 or 6 miles'.

The scale of these blast furnaces was described by Gerard Boate, a seventeenth century observer:

> This mouth [chimney] is not covered ... so that the flame ... may be seen a great way off in the night, and in the midst of the darkness maketh a terrible shew to travellers, who do not know what it is ... It is continually blown day and night without ceasing by two vast pair of bellows, the which ... rise and fall by turns, so that whilst the one pair of bellows doth swell and fill itself with wind, the other doth blow the same forth into the furnace.

They reached higher temperatures – up to 1,500°C – which produced molten iron. It would be released onto a bed of sand in which connecting channels were indented so it could flow freely until it cooled and solidified. Some believe the shapes of the cooled iron gave it its name – pig iron – because

The ruin of a round house, dating to around the sixth century AD, where iron objects were made. An excavation discovered pits, charcoal and iron residue, with corroded iron objects such as knives and nails. The well at the front was a source of water. The name attached to it long ago is St Gobnait's House, seemingly with reason, as her name is a derivative of gabha *('blacksmith' in Irish) and she is the patron saint of metalworkers. Ballyvourney, County Cork.*

Blast furnace at Furnace, County Mayo, built c.1738, where remnants from this busy site continue to work their way out of the soil. By-products of smelting are shown, including slag (on the left) and pig iron (on the right). The iron ore used here came from Srah in the nearby Partry Mountains.

they looked like a mother pig with her suckling babies latched on. In his book, written in the mid-seventeenth century, Gerard Boate describes how the great slabs of iron could weigh from one hundredweight (c.0.05 tons) to thirty hundredweight (c.1.5 tons) and how at that time, the workmen called them 'sowes'. They were then drawn by teams of oxen from the furnaces to the refineries, where huge hammers, also worked by water power, beat them free of their impurities, 'never ceasing from knocking day nor night'.

Charcoal, made from hardwood (usually oak) heated in a low-oxygen process to remove water and other compounds, was used to fuel blast furnaces, as it burned cleanly and reached consistent high temperatures. One acre of woodland was needed to make enough charcoal to produce two tons of iron. By the seventeenth century, our expansive Irish forests, the main fuel to operate these huge early blast furnaces, were a prime target for English settlers to plunder (including for export to England). Ironmasters applied regenerative woodland management skills in England, such as planting new trees or coppicing (where the trees are cut in such a way that they will regrow). But when they came to operate in Ireland, there is little evidence these methods were applied. Thus, by the eighteenth century our densely forested country was so depleted that, as Charles Smith wrote about Kerry in 1756, 'All, or the greater part of the hills, and mountains hereabouts, were formerly covered with trees, which have been destroyed by the Iron-works … when the workmen were obliged to stop smelting for want of charcoal.'

A model of a blast furnace showing the ramp for loading fuel and iron ore, and the building's two adjacent arches. The 'blowing arch' was where two sets of leather and wooden bellows operated, pumping out of sync with each other so that a steady rate of air flow was achieved. The 'tapping arch' was where first the waste and then the molten iron was tapped out, which flowed into moulds indented in sand, creating pig iron shapes. (Model crafted by Jake Justice Creations.)

The interior of the blast furnace chimney at Creevelea Ironworks, County Leitrim, where the surface shine is due to vitrification, a process in which intense heat transforms residue into a glass-like coating.

This plundering of natural resources impacted on wider Irish society, which depended on wood for the local economy, and yet the ironworks did not mitigate this in other ways. They were closely linked to colonisation and usually owned by English settlers who had been granted land under the plantation system, dispossessing Irish landowners. Thousands of English workers were imported, with some records suggesting that this was to conceal the method of iron production from the Irish, and there are records of some furnace owners being given licences to employ Irishmen until they could be replaced by Englishmen. Thus the ironworks became a symbol of English economic dominance and a target for Irish rebel activity, with many ironworks destroyed in the Irish rebellion of 1641.

With the depletion of the native forests and their supply of fuel, the industry waned. Eventually the fuel for blast furnaces was changed to coke, a refined form of coal, the supply of which was instrumental in fuelling the Industrial Revolution, as it allowed for mass production of iron and steel (essential for building railways and machinery). These coke-fired ironworks were on a massive scale; at the Creevelea Ironworks site, the incomplete remains of the furnace measures over six metres (twenty feet) high, and five and a half metres (eighteen feet) along each side. The works closed in 1896 – making this the last commercial iron smelting furnace in Ireland – with most of the buildings since demolished. Its huge furnace base is the only visible remnant not consumed by the undergrowth.

Blast furnace at Creevelea Ironworks, County Leitrim, near Sliabh an Iarainn (Iron Mountain), once a busy site. An advertisement in 1861 showcased its capability to produce around 150 tons of pig iron per week. It described how this site contained kilns, an engine house, ten workmen's cottages, a smithy and stabling for 30 horses. It was situated near ironstone beds (their raw material), peat bogs and coal mines (to supply fuel), and near Lough Allen (to transport their finished product by water).

Fair Day, Cahirciveen, County Kerry. In 1844, the fair in Cahirciveen was scheduled to be held in every month of the year, with two in September. Clothes sellers were a feature at fairs. (© National Library of Ireland.)

THE FUN OF THE FAIR

THE FAIR DAY

Irish people would excitedly anticipate the fair day, an important event in the local calendar. A dedicated area such as a fair green would be bustling throughout the day with people trading their animals or goods and catching up on the latest news. While a market was a smaller, more frequent affair for local people, the fair was a greater occasion where whole towns were taken over, attracting large crowds of people who travelled huge distances and had to be entertained, fed and accommodated. Fairs were often held on religious

Men and sheep on fair day at Leenane, County Galway. A newspaper article written in 1876 commemorated 15 August 1812 as the date the Leenane Fair or Pattern was founded as 'a meeting convened to afford the good and generous people of the West an opportunity of meeting in their thousands to spend a joyful day; and also as an inducement to their banished friends to come and rejoice or condole with the companions of their youth o'er past events'. (© Trinity College Dublin.)

Animal ramp, Borris, County Carlow, with a recreation of how it was used to load the animals into carts. In 1844, the fair in Borris was scheduled to be held in every month of the year except April, on the fair green seen behind the ramp, now a public park.

holidays or the feast days of the local saint (known as 'the pattern'), and if held at midsummer, a decorated pole as lofty as a ship's mast, called the *craebh*, was erected to form the central focus of the fair.

The result of a year's hard work on the land and fattening animals could be fulfilled at the fair. People would set out before dawn and travel for many miles, often on foot, while droving their animals. The sheer length of these journeys, and lack of any means of instant communication, meant the fair was always held on a set recurring date.

The right to hold each fair was granted by the Crown to a patentee (usually the local landlord), who was then responsible for running the fair and its

Taking toll at an Irish pig fair, 1890

infrastructure (often building the dedicated fair green, for example) and in exchange could charge a toll on every animal coming into the fair green. This right could be abused, however. One example noted in a parliamentary enquiry in 1856 was at Roscrea Fair, where a toll equating to 13 per cent of the sale price was charged on a goat – which was then seized when payment of the toll was refused.

The patentee's responsibility also extended to ensuring that weights and measures were accurate and in compliance with the standard set by parliament. The same enquiry found fraudulent weighing and bad practices including, in some places, men and women being placed into the market scales as weights. Specific importance was later put on having weighing machines available to weigh cattle.

There were certain traditions during the trading discussions. If the deal included female livestock, luck money (known as a luck-penny) which was believed to make the animal lucky in breeding, was paid to the buyer in addition to the sale price. As a sign that cattle had been sold, an area of their hair would be clipped, or a mark would be drawn on their back by a stick dipped in mud: a visible sign that they were off the market.

The atmosphere on the day was generally one of merriment. After the important trading business of the day had been completed (often involving a drink to seal the deal), people would enjoy the sideshows and games (including trials of strength), sing, dance, eat and drink, which often led to reported debauchery and fighting.

Beginning in the thirteenth century as a livestock market, the annual eight-day Donnybrook Fair in Dublin had by the early nineteenth century descended into a 'gigantic nuisance and national disgrace' with its violence and 'a mere drunken orgy'. Reports described the crowd's 'tumultuous excitement' in the densely crowded fair green, which was surrounded by a maddening discord

Weighing bridge, Fethard, County Tipperary

Animal ramp and pen, with an early twentieth-century cattle weighbridge still in situ. Ballindaggin, County Wexford.

of sounds from drums, bells, hawkers, and a dozen fiddlers and pipers playing away vigorously and independently. Pots of what was described as a 'hell-broth' boiled and bubbled over fires, suspended from a triangle, and the attendees drank alcohol until they sank off their seats in blissful unconsciousness. The nights descended into drunken chaos, with fighting becoming the leading characteristic of the fair. In fact, these activities caused the word 'donnybrook' to come into common usage to describe scenes of riot and disorder; it even entered the dictionary.

However, by 1840 things had improved, as witnessed by visitors to Ireland Mr and Mrs Hall (who had previously attended the more raucous version on a separate visit), who noted crowds of people amusing themselves, dancing in tents and gossiping, thronged side shows, and the crammed merry-go-round and hobby-horses. They theorised that this improvement was due to a more efficient police force and the temperance movement promoting sobriety. The Church of the Sacred Heart, completed in 1866, overlooked the old fair green, and was celebrated as a temple 'raised to God's worship on the place where demons had received sacrifices'.

The influence of temperance was also seen at Finglas in Dublin. The revellers there crowned a 'Queen of the May' at their May fair and among the games were competitions to catch a soapy shaved pig, to catch (while blindfolded) a running bell-ringer, to make the most fetching grin through a horse-collar, and to climb a greased maypole to reach prizes. In 1842, however, a Catholic priest, Father Henry Young, a key figure in the temperance movement, cut down and burned the maypole and the following year burned the fiddles and bagpipes of the revellers at the fair.

Some fairs have their own unique traditions even to this day. For reasons lost to time, at the centuries-old Puck Fair in Killorglin, County Kerry, to signal the start of the festivities a wild goat is caught and crowned King Puck, and reigns over the fair on an elevated platform until released back into the wild when the festivities end.

Donnybrook Fair, Dublin, 1847, where 'crime and disorder held potent sway' for some time. The tents were made by driving wattles into the earth in two parallel rows, turning down and tying them together, and covering with cloth.

THE PATTERN DAY

Most parishes in Ireland have a patron saint, or *patrún* in Irish, whose feast day is celebrated on what was known as the pattern day, which had the main features of a fair but with an additional religious element. The focus was usually the holy well dedicated to the saint. These wells, sacred since ancient times, became important sites of assembly and veneration following the destruction of Catholic churches.

Usually work would not take place on the feast day, or special rules around working applied; for example, in County Kerry and west County Cork, work that required the turning of wheels (milling, spinning, etc.) was avoided, and people walked long distances rather than cycle. They would make an extra effort for the pattern, ironing their clothes and polishing their shoes the night before. Sometimes, in the excitement of the day, a runaway marriage might even take place.

A pilgrim at a holy well, Doon, County Donegal. (Photograph taken between 1860 and 1883, © National Library of Ireland.)

St Brigid's Shrine, Faughart, County Louth, the reputed birthplace of St Brigid in the fifth century. Pilgrims would visit the ancient stones as part of their rounds, now numbered in the order they were to be visited. The prayers for the Knee Stone (right), which marks the spot where the saint is reputed to have knelt to pray, were the Pater, Ave and Gloria. At the Head Stone (left), where the pilgrims would place their head into the white circle, one Ave was due. Note the offerings tied to the tree on the left.

Lady's Well, Titeskin, County Cork (see also page pages 180–181). This carving of the Blessed Virgin Mary with a halo is one of the stations for doing the rounds and the deep crosses have been incised by thousands of pilgrims scraping it with a stone. The text reads 'Seven Pater Nosters and Seven Ave Marias. The Honour 1731'. An account from 1893 recorded 'blind men praying, and boys who used to kiss a rude figure cut on the stone in relief'. The other side of the stone is visible on page 181.

St Finbarr's Oratory, Gougane Barra, County Cork, where two huge patterns took place each year in honour of St John and St Finbarr (the latter is said to have lived as a hermit on this island). The cattle would be driven into the lake to swim, and the ropes used to tie them hung at the pilgrimage site afterwards as protection against disease. A visitor in the early nineteenth century described the riot of the pattern, its mixture of piety and blasphemy, and how a beggar was scraping a cross into the wall (which was at that point about two inches deep) with small pieces of slate, which were sold to the pilgrims.

Each well had a different tradition for pilgrims to complete their holy 'rounds': some involved walking clockwise around the well itself a set number of times; at others there was a sequence of stops at different points called 'stations'. At each station, pilgrims would recite set prayers, such as a certain number of Paters (Pater Noster/Our Father) and Aves (Ave Maria/Hail Mary), hoping that the favours they were praying for would be granted by the saint. These rounds could be done on any day, but were considered more potent if completed on the saint's feast day. An offering would be made, such as a coin, rosary beads, or a rag, often dipped in the water of the well or a bullaun stone,

Mám Éan, Connemara, County Galway, as depicted in a sketch in 1842: a pilgrimage site predating Christianity but dedicated to St Patrick from the fifth century. The site had an altar used to celebrate secret masses in the Penal times, a holy well and stations. A great pattern day took place in July/August each year, with crowds descending to attend mass and do the rounds. The cave-like recess on the hill is known as St Patrick's Bed, where the saint is said to have slept, and circles of stone represent the stations. There are tents set up in the centre, and there appears to be a faction fight depicted in the background on the right, a sight witnessed and recorded by Henry Inglis, a visitor here in 1834. (Engraving by H. Griffiths after a picture by W. H. Bartlett.)

and tied to the sacred tree. Anyone who took another person's offering in ill will was believed to catch the disease of the person for whom the offering had been made. The process was finished off with a sip of the holy water, and some of the water might be brought home for protection or healing. The three key features of these sites were intrinsically linked in the belief of the people: the sacred water, the venerated tree and the stones.

Animal health was also catered for: people brought home water in jars for their cattle (it would be administered into their nostrils or ears) or drove their horses or cattle into a pool or river to swim in the belief they would not last the year without this drenching.

The pattern day involved the sacred and the profane, with religious activities sitting alongside courting and fun. Drinking and fighting were also a feature. At a nineteenth-century pattern held in Kilmainham in Dublin, which venerated St John, pilgrims drank whiskey mixed with the holy well's 'saintly waters' and there were numerous incidents of fighting.

Many factors influenced the decline of the pattern. Penal Laws in the early eighteenth century had prohibited Catholics assembling, including at holy wells, and then during the Great Hunger in the 1840s, festivals went unobserved and traditions neglected when starvation stalked the country. The excessive drinking and fighting in the following years caused many Catholic and temperance interventions, and by the 1930s many local records were referencing their area's pattern as part of their village's history rather than its present.

FACTION FIGHTING

Large gatherings of people across much of Ireland in the eighteenth and nineteenth century were almost guaranteed to end in an organised faction

Gravestone in Ballindaggin, County Wexford, which reads 'Here lies the Body of James Cowman who was Inhumanly murdered on Moneyhore march 25th 1828 ag'd 24 yr'. Moneyhore Fair was the location of what was described as a riot on that date, and Cowman and another man were severely beaten with cudgels.

fight, with one lawyer, a Mr Jebb, boldly stating during a murder trial in 1814, 'I believe a fight makes an essential part of an Irish fair.' The fights could involve frightful savagery; one faction fight in Kerry resulted in at least twenty deaths. Murders from faction fighting were 'the most numerous class of cases at most Irish assizes' (courts), with frequent newspaper reports in the nineteenth century resigned to the fights' bloody outcomes as 'the usual melancholy results'. Yet there are witnesses who said that sometimes after the fights, the opponents could civilly shake hands with no bad blood between them.

The 'battlefields' were usually at busy fair greens and marketplaces, though other public gatherings such as patterns, races or funerals could also attract a fight. A French traveller to Ireland in the 1790s witnessed how mourners at a funeral procession argued over which side of the family the deceased woman should be buried with, deposited the coffin carrier on the street 'and commenced a vigorous fight to determine by blows of sticks to which side the remains should be carried'. Faction fights might also be organised by the supporters of political causes, after evictions, or the result of disputes between those on the side of boycotted landlords and those boycotting.

Plaque commemorating a huge faction fight at Ballyeagh Strand, south of Ballybunion, County Kerry in 1834, involving several thousand people, and resulting in the deaths of at least twenty people (as recorded, but it is believed the number was significantly higher) who were beaten with sticks and hurleys, stoned, and pursued into the river, where many drowned while fighting for their lives. In the weeks following the fight, three fighters of the faction of the Lawlers, who had been arrested, were 'brutally murdered by a party of the peasantry' while being conveyed to Tralee Gaol.

Irish blackthorn seller, carrying his lot of seasoned blackthorn sticks

Whatever the main event, after the bustle of the day's activities an atmosphere of expectation would come over the crowd, rather like sports spectators today. Formed by allegiances (to villages, families or parishes) that passed from father to son, each faction had a name, for example the Black Hens or the Magpies, and a leader. One leader would issue a challenge to the other by trailing his coat on the ground. If the other man took up the challenge, he would stand on the coat. Then there would be a fierce and generally bloody encounter, lasting for hours. Hundreds or even thousands of men would fight with sticks, stones, fists and sometimes guns. The fighters might form lines of attack, which surged forward and retreated, and the cracking of sticks, sounding like gunfire, would be followed by screeching, bellowing and moaning. Several men could be fighting one man at a time even if he was on the ground, with no restraint around cracking skulls (the men lined their hats with straw to give some protection). Women were known to assist by filling an old stocking with stones to swing at the heads of their faction's opponents, but were never intentionally struck by the men.

The battles were often organised by agreement in advance, allowing time to prepare weapons and practise fighting skills. A special form of stick fighting had developed, complete with trainers who instructed learners how to hold the stick about a third of the way from the slender end, which protected their elbow, and with the thumb forward on the stick for control. A second, shorter stick could be used in the other hand as a shield. Even the children would practise stick fighting with each other.

Early accounts refer to fighting sticks as shillalah or shillelah (now more commonly spelt shillelagh, with a nineteenth-century record stating they were named after the wood in Wicklow where 'the best oaks and black thorns were grown'), kippeens, clehalpeens (or simply alpeen), etc. Many faction fighters kept special sticks for the sole purpose of fighting, and even named their sticks – one such example being 'Death without the Priest'. Much effort was put into selecting the wood (from blackthorn, ash, oak, or hazel), then seasoning and straightening the stick to make the perfect fighting stick, about the length of a walking stick. Then shorter cudgels might be made. A local history account

Stick fighter. Illustration by Erskine Nichol (1825–1904).

St Gobnait's Well, which featured in a story published in 1847 in which a faction leader had to reach the stone, stand on it, and wave his hat three times with three distinct cheers before their faction would be declared the winner. The top of the 'beehive-like and partially corbelled' stone structure (according to the National Monuments Service) has been paved over and pointed. Ballyvourney, County Cork.

from County Leitrim records how they used the tough main stem of a sapling ash, which they cut to around 16 inches long, inserted a hot poker four inches into the pith, and filled the resulting hollow with lead. To prevent it splitting on impact, the end would be covered with a wax-end used in boot-making, or stitched leather like that on sliotars (hurling balls). These modified sticks were known as loaden butts, and the weighted end caused maximum injury. There is also an account of a hurley bound with wire being used. The fighters would secure their sticks around their wrists with leather thongs as fat as a finger so they could not be knocked out of their hands.

Some men became highly skilled with these sticks. A story from County Leitrim tells that after a challenge at a fair in Ballinamore in the 1830s, a man named Dan Boyle from Ardrum used a blackthorn stick to break pieces off an officer's sword with each blow he struck, and to knock all the buttons off the officer's uniform. The officer, accepting defeat, said he never imagined that any man could attain such a feat with a blackthorn stick, and paid tribute to Dan's skill and restraint. A character called Connor O'Callaghan in William Carleton's nineteenth-century short story, who had broken two skulls in his fighting days, was described as a powerful *bulliah battha* (translated as 'cudgel-player' in the author's footnote), who never met a man able to fight him.

A newspaper from 1847 tells the story of a faction fight held thirty years previously, which was organised annually in Ballyvourney, County Cork. The winner would be the faction leader who managed to get to St Gobnait's

An aerial view of the site where the faction fighters in the 1847 story did their rounds before their fight, which included the station shown at the front. Known as St Gobnait's Grave, it is an ancient cairn of stones, covered in sod, with a stone slab on top. St Gobnait's Well is out of frame at the rear. Ballyvourney, County Cork.

Well (described as a mossy stone in the centre of the 'field of battle'), stand on it, wave his hat three times, and give three distinct cheers. So when the men had paid their devotions to their parish's patron saint and 'given their rounds at her holy well', they fought for 'the honour and glory' of their faction until 'the soft, green turf soon became slippery with blood'. Having won for two years in a row, the Hurlys' leader (with his 'long hair, which sixty winters had whitened, waving in the mountain breeze') had issued his first cheer from the stone when a man from the rival Riley faction shot him through the neck. Hurly grabbed a handful of moss from the stone, rammed it into his own wound to absorb the blood and carried on to win the fight, the others now frozen in awestricken wonder, and walked six miles home to dig his potatoes, saying 'I wouldn't give them the satisfaction to say they hurt me.' It is unclear whether this story was factual or written for entertainment, but it included a footnote stressing that the physician who witnessed the scene at Hurly's house was still living and frequently related the story of what he had witnessed.

Most Irish people were living in dire conditions with little hope of rising out of poverty, and one newspaper theorised about faction fighting that 'Such a savage pastime is a pretty instance of the rumoured depressed state of the farming class in Kerry.' While the faction fight was a way for fighters to display their skills, it was also a way of resolving disputes (such as land disputes, family honour, etc.) without involving the British courts. Irish people generally viewed the courts with warranted suspicion, as they did not generally get justice in this legal system. On one point all factions were in agreement: the police were to be kept completely in the dark as to the names of those involved.

This 'infighting' of the Irish people also suited the authorities, who for a period didn't really intervene as long as the fighting was kept contained within the factions. News reports often recorded how the authorities in attendance had been on a break at the time or had left for the night before the fight broke out. Ultimately, the division of the local people into factions deflected attention from the actions of the authorities.

Handball playing in Ireland, Illustrated Sporting and Dramatic News, *1884*

outer layer, such as sheepskin. These original older balls, known as hardballs (prior to the introduction of rubber balls in the twentieth century), needed to be hit forcefully and made the game a test of strength as well as skill and stamina.

Across Ireland, there are ruins of ancient churches and monasteries, most destroyed during the dissolution of the monasteries by Henry VIII, and the locals used what remained of their standing walls to play handball. There were also purpose-built ball alleys.

Grangefertagh Church, County Kilkenny, a thirteenth-century church on a monastic site, which was converted into a ball alley after it fell into disuse from 1780

Secret rebel activity sometimes took place in the shelter of ball alley walls. In the run-up to the 1798 Rebellion, meetings of the United Irishmen in County Kildare were disguised as matches in ball alleys. In County Louth, Michael Boylan, a young rebel leader, was arrested in Collon while playing handball and hanged in public in Drogheda one hour after receiving his sentence, his sister chancing upon the distressing scene while out shopping.

A century later, the Irish Volunteers drilled in the secrecy of ball alley walls. To counter this, in the years leading up to the War of Independence, the British authorities required permits for any handball matches so as to limit gatherings there, and on occasion they intimidated or prevented people playing. In 1920, to avoid drawing the attention of the patrolling Black and Tans (the auxiliary British force known for their brutal attacks), the crowd

Memorial plaque to the Carnew Massacre of the 1798 rebellion, when local men being held at the British army base at Carnew Castle from a previous battle were marched to the local ball alley and executed. Note the pikes, the main weapon used by the rebels, depicted in the lower half of the plaque. Carnew, County Wicklow.

Ball alley in Ullard, County Kilkenny, where the ninth-century high cross (bottom right of photograph) became a bone of contention between the players and antiquarians who were trying to move it to preserve it. 'The people again objected because it prevented them from playing ball. So it was put standing at the back of the alley upon a ditch where the spectators used to sit when there was a handball match. So it was brought back to its old place and there it remains to this day.' Spectators probably stood on planks of wood laid across the concrete plinths to its rear, which could be accessed via a set of stone steps on the right-hand wall.

at the exciting All-Ireland Championship in Limerick had to be warned by the organisers to keep silent throughout the game, with the referee calling the scores in a hushed voice. This must have been a challenge, since ball alley galleries were always full for the big matches and there was plenty of side betting, meaning plenty of vocal enthusiasm for the game.

Handball was popular with the authorities, and many police barracks had a ball alley attached for their own use, as had Catholic seminaries. However, not all clergy leadership were as enthusiastic. In County Fermanagh in 1843 it was noted that the clergy had broken up bands of 'idle youths' who were caught playing handball on the sabbath, only for them to progress to playing cards behind haystacks, with the magistrate personally getting involved in checking out these meeting places. It was also popular in the confined spaces of prisons, as seen in the experiences of republican prisoners in English jails in the early twentieth century (hurling was banned, as the hurley could be used as a weapon).

Interior of ball alley, Ullard, County Kilkenny. The twelfth-century church's walls were converted into a ball alley at some time prior to 1839 and spectators vied for the best views through the old monastery's lancet windows.

Ball alley in a cemetery in Owning, County Kilkenny, adjoining the ruins of a twelfth-century church

Lifting stones to build walls on Inis Mór, County Galway. Photograph by Heinrich Becker. (© National Folklore Collection, UCD.)

Fierce rivalries also developed, even internationally. In the late nineteenth century, Irish and American players vied to be declared the champion of the world, with large sums (up to several hundred pounds) wagered.

At this time, there was no standard for the ball, the court, or the game itself. Handball rules were formalised by the Gaelic Athletic Association, which had been set up when Ireland was still under British rule to make athletics more accessible to a larger audience and cultivate and preserve our national pastimes. The popularity of handball swept the country in the twentieth century, with Gaelic handball alleys built in schools and institutions across the country. Many are now disused, but their standing walls are an important reminder of the esteem in which this traditional sport was held in Ireland.

STONE LIFTING

Stone lifting was an ancient competitive tradition carried out in Irish rural communities, but from the mid-nineteenth century, broadly in line with the years following the Great Hunger, Irish people generally forgot this test of strength. The people of Ireland had been physically strong from manual labour (including clearing rocky fields, building stone walls, hauling nets heaving with fish and carrying loads) and would hold stone-lifting contests at weddings and funerals. Those who succeeded in lifting these stones became local heroes for their great feat of strength, and the stones were often named after them. Indeed, Irish lifting stones are said to be the heaviest compared to other countries' traditions. Our tradition goes back to ancient Irish legends, several of which reference mythological heroes lifting and throwing giant stones. It is also deeply embedded in our language through an old Irish saying, *Is é mo chloch nirt é*, which translates to 'It is my stone of strength' and was used in the context of 'It is as much as I can do'.

The height of the Irish lift depended on the legend surrounding each particular stone, with some only requiring it to be lifted a little off the ground, others requiring a lift to the knee, lap or chest, and some requiring special tasks, such as lifting it onto a wall or altar.

The Lonergan Stone, about 177.5kg, Shanrahan Cemetery, Clogheen, County Tipperary. Thomas Lonergan was the strongest man in the parish of Clogheen around the late nineteenth century, and many came after mass to challenge him to lift the local stone.

In some locations there were also special challenges. At Disert graveyard in County Donegal, where special smaller stones sit on an outdoor altar, as a test of male virility the local tradition is to lift one stone with each hand, holding them from the top, and carry them from the outdoor altar to the well and back again three times. In Fahy graveyard in County Leitrim, overlooking Lough Allen, generations of men tested their strength after burials by lifting a pot-shaped stone straight up off the ground without being allowed to turn it to find a better grip, a rule that increased the difficulty of the lift. The local story traces strong men lifting this stone back to at least the Great Hunger.

In the 1930s, folklore recorded that 'on the cross roads of Owning there is a big tree surrounded with stones and it is called the bulk'. Famine relief was distributed every day on the bulk. In more recent times, locals recount how the large stone on the bulk, about 120kg, was fixed into place for safety, as men coming out of the local pub were attempting to lift it. It has since been released from its constraints, and the challenge includes walking around the tree while carrying it. Owning, County Kilkenny.

Mullán Phort Bhéal an Dúin, with the hill fort Dún Aonghasa in the background, on Inis Mór, Aran Islands, County Galway. This stone was described in 'The Stone' as 'a round block of granite. It sparkled as the sunshine shone on the particles of mica in its surface. It lay on the ground, on a clear space between the rocks. All round it there were bruised stones, bruised to a powder and where it lay there was a little hollow.'

David Keohane, Irish historical stone finder and lifter, located this stone, Mullán Phort Bhéal an Dúin, which weighs about 171kg.

Some stones are special indeed, and written about by our great writers. In Liam O'Flaherty's short story 'The Stone', he tells of an old man whose body had shrunk so his clothes hung loose upon him, remembering his youth and seeking out, to lift one last time, a stone that 'from time immemorial it had been the custom of the young men of the village to test their strength by lifting it':

> It was a great day in each young man's life when he raised the stone from the ground and 'gave it wind', as they said. And if he raised it to his knees, he was a champion, the equal of the best. And if he raised it to his chest he was a hero, a phenomenon of strength and men talked of him. Whereas, he who failed to lift it from the ground became the butt of everybody's scorn. It had always been so, from the time of the most remote ancestors of the people.

Garadice Lake and Drumreilly Church of Ireland church, Lower Drumreilly, County Leitrim. Inside sits an ancient carved apex stone, which could be the stone in the story. This told how an apex stone from the medieval church on Church Island was taken to Lower Drumreilly as a marker for a grave. The current church was built on the site of an earlier Catholic church and therefore people of the Catholic faith are also buried in its graveyard.

The medieval church on Church Island, Garadice Lake, County Leitrim, with its apex stone missing (the apex stone is the top stone at roof level in a gable end, usually triangular). This church was originally constructed in the thirteenth century, with further development in the fifteenth century.

A story in our National Folklore Collection, written in the 1930s, tells of a stone of antiquity being used as a lifting stone in previous generations. It says that the apex stone from the medieval church on Church Island in Garadice Lake had been brought to Lower Drumreilly as a grave marker and at funerals men would lift this stone. It was described as 'carved and ornamented' and 'not very heavy but owing to the way it had to be lifted, very few could do it. It had a hollow on each side, and into those two hollows the lifters had to put the heel of their hands, and press their knees against their hands, and lift

A carved and ornamented apex stone in Drumreilly Church of Ireland church, County Leitrim

The Cloughundra, about 188kg. Aughagower, County Mayo. Folklore records that the holes in the stone are the trace of a giant's fingers, who used to throw it over his shoulder as a man would throw a pebble.

the stone in that position.' The story, which was told by a grandfather to his grandson, could date the tradition around this particular stone to before the Great Hunger.

Studies continue and have yet to ascertain fully why the practice died out, but many believe it is due to the impact of the Great Hunger. The people's focus was on staying alive, so many aspects of Irish culture ceased during this time, including sports and pastimes. After unimaginable suffering, emigration and societal changes, this practice was eventually forgotten, and these stones often lie in graveyards, untouched since their last lift.

However, a revival of the tradition in recent years means these sleeping stones are being reawakened to be lifted once again.

Cloch an Chathaoir Dhearg (Stone of the Red Chair), about 203kg. Red Chair Crossroads, County Cork.

CURES

Lady's Well (also known as Whitewell), Titeskin, Aghada, County Cork. Late nineteenth/early twentieth century.

STONES

Belief in the curative power of stones was part of everyday life in Ireland. Children who had warts would put as many pebbles as they had warts in a bag and leave it at the crossroads, the place where a passerby was most likely to pick it up, in the belief that the stones would transfer the warts to the person who found them. Or if a person had a pain in their side, it would disappear if they bent down to lift up a stone, spat under it, and left it down again in the

Cloch an Phoill (the 'hole stone'), Aghade, County Carlow. Infants were passed through the hole (which is about 33cm) to be cured of rickets.

The Petrified Dairy (also known as the Rolls of Butter), St Feaghna's Graveyard, Garranes, County Kerry.

same position. Stones would be taken from the walls of old church ruins and brought home, in the belief that they could cure aches and pains.

Then there are the sacred stones at special sites, from simple holed stones to stone tables and stone seats. People believed their curative properties derived from their unique origins, whether supernatural events, the coming of Christianity, an Irish legend or just because they had an unusual shape.

The large hole in Cloch an Phoill (meaning the 'hole stone') gave rise to a tradition of passing infants through it to cure them of rickets. The granite stone is thought to have originally been set in place in the early Bronze Age (up to 3,000 years ago) to mark a burial. Some think the purpose of the hole was for people to pass food to their loved one in the other world. Tradition records that the stone is associated with the High Kings of Ireland; it is where Niall of the Nine Hostages, the fifth-century ancestor of the Uí Néill Kings of Tara, tied up his enemy, Eochu, by running a chain through the hole. Eochu broke free, leaving marks on the stone, killed the nine warriors Niall had sent to kill him, and eventually killed Niall.

In Kerry, it is believed that when St Feaghna caught a dairymaid stealing, he turned her and her dairy to stone (now known as the Petrified Dairy). The five basin-like hollows are supposed to be keelers (bowl-shaped milk coolers) and her butter is the oval stones (the form that butter used to be shaped into). Her dasher (long-handled paddle) and churn were also turned into stone.

Mad Chair of Dunany, County Louth, also known as the Madman's Chair and as Cathaoir Áine

A round stone (said to be agate) called the Bulla or St Gobnait's Bowl, believed to have healing properties. It is wedged into a niche in the wall of a ruined church and rubbed by the pilgrim doing the rounds at St Gobnait's holy well in Ballyvourney, County Cork. Legend has it that St Gobnait used it as a throwing weapon to knock down an unwelcome building under construction nearby (a pagan temple, a Protestant church or a tyrant's castle, depending on the version of the story), and it returned to her each time.

The churn's lid was found in the field in later times and placed back onto the stone. (This lid is the quern in the centre of the stone that was found in the nineteenth century.) The dairymaid herself tried to escape but he turned her into a human-sized standing stone, with a hawthorn growing beside her, about midway up the opposite hillside. It was believed impossible to remove the stones from the 'dairy'. A young shop boy tried this, but his horse refused to let him ride away. Due to local superstition the same stones have remained in place for thousands of years. They show signs of wear and it was thought the rock may have been used for domestic purposes (for example grinding) before a sacred use was attached to it, first pagan and then Christian. In more recent centuries, it was one of the stations of the rounds at this site.

St Ronan's Altar, Kilronan, County Roscommon, with St Lasair's Well in the background

Pilgrims would seek a cure for warts by circling the rock seven times in an anti-clockwise direction, reciting a Pater and an Ave at each of the 'butter rolls', and making the sign of the cross on the warts with the water from the rock. Others believed the stones were turned to put curses on people.

Another supernatural origin is found at the Mad Chair of Dunany. In Irish legend, the fairy queen (or sometimes goddess) Áine lived in a fort (*dún*) on the headland above the chair. The name of the area, Dunany, comes from Dún Áine. The reef stretching out into the sea is the start of a causeway to Scotland or England that she had begun to build, but she sat down on the stone seat and became mad. In another version, an English fairy turned her into the actual stone chair. The tradition around the chair is that 'all the distraught in mind were wont to be attracted as to a lodestone' (magnetised rock). Folklore research from 1852 tells us that if a mentally ill person 'seated themselves thrice upon it ... they became incurable'. Alternatively, if a sane person sat on the chair, they might also 'become subject to the power of Áine, that is, become affected with lunacy'.

Then there are the stones whose stories tell of special qualities derived from the coming of Christianity. Embedded in the wall in Fenloe Graveyard, County Clare, there is a plague stone said to have been blessed by the sixth-century St Luchtigern to cure people with cholera. Those afflicted would rub their legs on the stone and make the sign of the cross. Later, and even to the present day, pilgrims do the same to seek a cure for swollen joints.

St Ronan's Altar is a slab believed to have been used by the saint to celebrate mass and later used to celebrate secret masses during Penal times. The top of the stone table is pitted all over, perhaps man-made marks, perhaps natural,

St Patrick's Chair, Altadaven, County Tyrone

Outside Grallagh Cemetery in Garristown, County Dublin, sits St Patrick's Stone, believed to have been where the saint tethered his horse through the hole that runs through to the other side. It was said that if St Patrick's action of placing his fingers into the stone's five holes were replicated, sore hands would be cured. Lying with your back pressed against the stone was believed to cure backache. Love beliefs were also attached to this stone: if a man reached through the hole and grasped a woman's hand, she would be his love for the rest of their lives. The council's road workers removed the stone at one stage without realising its significance, but following local opposition replaced it in the road.

The Tomb of the Jealous Man and Woman lies in the ruin of the medieval Newtown parish church near Trim, County Meath. The sword lying between Sir Lucas Dillon and his first wife, Lady Jane Bathe, was said to keep them separated. Numerous rusty pins cluster across the top of the tomb, as visitors were supposed to aid them in the good work (earning salvation) by dropping a pin on the tomb. It is believed to the current day that rubbing a pin on a wart and leaving it on the tomb will cure the wart, which will fade away as the pin rusts away.

and its rugged edge is supposedly where a nineteenth-century bishop who disapproved of the behaviour of the people at the pattern day organised for it to be smashed into two pieces in front of the crowd. The second piece has never been recovered. In the belief that the table would cure their back pain, pilgrims would crawl underneath it three times, making a cross shape with their movements. Some went further, turning the stone on top clockwise and praying at the adjacent St Lasair's Well, which was said to cure sore eyes.

The forested glen in Altadaven, County Tyrone where St Patrick's Chair sits with its unusual formation of rocks, is, according to tradition, sacred to the pre-Christian rites of Druidism. Later, St Patrick is said to have driven demons over the cliff here ('demons' might refer to the druids) and preached

Rusty pins and other offerings on the Tomb of the Jealous Man and Woman

the gospel from the chair to the people on the slope below. Down this hillside, underneath the stone seat, is a bullaun stone with a water-filled depression. It is referred to as a well, yet no source of water can be traced. Folklore attributes this magical appearance to St Patrick drawing water from the stone; even on the driest day, it has never run dry, and as often as it is emptied, the water will quickly fill up to the same level again. Offerings seeking cures have been left on rag trees and placed carefully into the many little caves and indentations throughout the site. Blaeberry (bilberry) Sunday was celebrated here at the end of July each year. A young girl, Bridget Sherlock, recorded in the 1930s what she was told by an older relative about the scene: 'crowds and crowds of boys and girls all enjoying themselves, laughing, courting, singing, and dancing, some picking the ripe blae-berries, some climbing up to see St. Patricks altar and chair, all wearing happy faces and enjoying themselves to their hearts' content'. Their fun included sitting on the stone chair and making a wish, which they believed would come true.

WATER

Ireland's ancient wells are sacred places, sites of devotion and faith that are steeped in the traditions that have come down from our ancestors through the centuries. These natural springs are most often in peaceful locations, ancient sanctuaries where personal devotion can take place or healing be sought to cure an ailment.

Wells, rivers and other water bodies were venerated in early Irish history. Stories tell of water being the portal to another world, the unearthly place

St Brigid's Well, Faughart Old Graveyard, County Louth, where local folklore recorded that a cure for headaches was to drink the well's water out of a skull that used to lie beside the well. Drinking water from a human skull to cure toothache is recorded at other sites.

of the fairies, gods and goddesses, a busy world where activities resembling those in our land are carried out. Archaeological evidence supports this oral history: votive offerings such as weapons and treasures have been found in water, a practice designed to honour deities and seek their favour. In Irish legend water is deeply sacred and a source of knowledge, frequently linked to goddesses or powerful female figures. The origin legends of two large Irish rivers, the Shannon and the Boyne, both involve women visiting magic wells, where rivers then burst forth, and Sinann and Boann, respectively, became the goddesses of those rivers.

It is commonly understood that Ireland's sacred or holy wells date from prehistoric times, but from the fifth century they became Christianised, with the early Christian saints assimilating with the existing pagan veneration to baptise converts at the wells. The origin stories of many of our wells date to these times, when the well is recalled as having burst forth when a saint thrust their staff into the ground. The water was regarded as almost sentient; if it was offended, say by clothes being washed in it, it would dry up and spring up somewhere else.

Holy wells were visited all year round, but their healing or curative properties were believed to be particularly potent on their associated pattern day – the feast day of the patron saint of the local area – or the evening before. This involved the people 'paying the rounds' at stations and there was a focus on the curative (or protective) properties of the water at the well, frequently in conjunction with a sacred tree or stone. At the site, people would usually drink the water or rub it on an affected body part. Wells associated with eye cures were common, presumably because bathing the eyes with clean fresh water would be beneficial for eye infections in times when running water wasn't generally available in homes and eyes were particularly irritated by the smoke from turf (peat) fires. A visitor to Gougane Barra in 1813 described how the well was crowded to excess, with the people thrusting body parts that had disgusting sores on them into the water, and others bottling the same water to be taken away and sold. Water from holy wells was used to bless homes, fields and boats. Fishermen would place a bottle of the water in their boats

St Moling's Well, St Mullins, County Carlow

St Hugh's Well, Clerhanbeg, Ballinaglera, County Leitrim, which fills with iron-rich water from Sliabh an Iarainn (Iron Mountain), causing its bright colouring and a furry deposit on the stones in the well

when they went fishing or undertook a voyage. If a fish – usually a trout, eel or salmon (a sacred symbol in Irish mythology and in Christianity) – was spotted in the well, this would bring even more potency to its cure. It was believed to have supernatural qualities too – water from a holy well would never boil.

In Kerry, at Tobar na nGealt ('Well of the Mad'), people suffering from mental illness were reputed to gain great benefit from staying in the area to avail of the water regularly, which was believed to cure mental illness, and returned home sane and in good health.

At St Moling's Well, the tradition is that the water from the well is said to cure ailments of the head in particular, especially when poured over the head and when imbibed, although it is also believed to cure the mind and areas of the body it is applied to. A pool of seven springs feeds into a stone font in the remains of a roofless baptismal chapel dated to around AD 1100. Local tradition records that St Moling himself dug out a mill race (a channel to control water to turn a millwheel) for his seventh-century monastery's mill, and then consecrated it. The ritual for pilgrims to follow includes entering the stream (into which the well flows) barefoot and walking against the flow of the water back towards the blessed well. Thousands of people waded through these waters during the Black Death in the mid-fourteenth century to benefit from the water's healing qualities. Plague may have been associated with St Moling because he was a healing saint (he healed lepers and cripples); more pertinently, he had suffered from ulcers on his feet, and ulcers were a symptom of the plague. This belief, over a thousand years old, still lives on, with bottles of the water going to local hospitals and the Irish diaspora requesting the water be sent all over the world. (Note also the 'Blessed Clay' section below, which details the cure for toothache when the water from this well is mixed with the local blessed clay.)

St Dymphna's Well, Kildownet, Achill Island, County Mayo. There are adjacent church ruins, with a cemetery containing large areas of unmarked graves of those who died in the Great Hunger.

In County Leitrim, St Hugh's Well remains continuously filled with iron-rich water from Sliabh an Iarainn (Iron Mountain), which is what gives the water its reddish-brown or orange colour. It is believed to cure mental confusion or bewilderment, which possibly aligns with some symptoms of iron deficiency. An iron-rich well is known as a chalybeate (an old English word for iron-rich), and many chalybeate waters became popular to drink at spas across Ireland in the eighteenth century, and their waters were sold in chemist shops for their health and medicinal properties.

St Dymphna's Well on Achill Island is a tidal well close to the water's edge and adjacent to where St Dymphna founded a church here in the seventh century. The local tradition is that Dymphna had escaped to Achill because her father wanted to marry her himself after her mother died. To prevent this marriage, she had prayed for (and been granted) a skin disease that would

Lady's Well (also known as Whitewell), Titeskin, Aghada, County Cork. Late nineteenth century/early twentieth century.

Lady's Well (Whitewell), Titeskin, Aghada, County Cork. Pilgrims incised a cross with a loose stone (visible on the upright stone)

disfigure her face, but once on the island she washed her face in water from this well and became beautiful again. She then went to Belgium, but her father tracked her down and decapitated her. St Dymphna is the patron saint of people with mental illness. The first person at the well at sunrise has the best chance of having their prayers answered.

At Lady's Well in Titeskin, County Cork, a huge ash tree has stood over the well for centuries, its roots slowly pushing through the stones of the whitewashed wall. Previously known as Whitewell, it was popular with people from all over the country who sought spiritual and physical healing; a busy place of pilgrimage, particularly in the mid-nineteenth century, when hundreds of people attended the pattern day, praying and bathing in the water. A magic trout was reportedly a feature to be spotted in the clear water

Pilgrims at a holy well in Galway c.1870. This has been identified as St Augustine's Well by O'Dowd in his Holy Wells of Galway City.

of this well and there are several stories of people being cured here, including a crippled man who washed his legs in the water flowing away from the well and was able to leave his crutches under the tree. Similarly, the parents of a young boy who was unable to walk washed his legs and he was instantly cured; his father vowed to visit the well every pattern day as long as he lived. A woman who was cured of deafness arranged what was described as a beautiful statue of Our Lady, three feet high and in a concrete shelter.

St Augustine's Well, on the shores of Lough Atalia in Galway city, has been in existence for hundreds of years, but there is a debate over whether the current well is in the exact location of the original well. It is a freshwater well, even though it sits in a tidal area. In 1673, a fourteen-year-old boy was recorded as being cured at St Augustine's Well. When he was brought there he was so close to death that his coffin had already been made. He was suffering from a vomiting condition, which meant he could not hold food down over a long period, and had been diagnosed as incurable. He was submerged in the water and woke up claiming that he had seen a religious vision and was to drink the water. He drank three draughts in the name of the Holy Trinity, then got up and walked around the well. He continued drinking the water for nine days afterwards, and then was said to be cured. This incident was taken so seriously that there was an investigation into it. The well is quiet now, but at one time so many people visited that carts would line the road beside it. It was known particularly for curing eye ailments, but general ailments were also cured. One woman remembered her mother pointing out the crutches and walking sticks left there by people who had been cured. The tradition is to walk around the well in bare feet while saying prayers.

St Augustine's Well, Galway City

Chink Well in the caves at Portrane, County Dublin, where the sea surrounds the hollow of the well at high tide but the water in the well remains fresh and crystal clear. The bright colouring is due to the growth of red algae on the rocks.

When Catholics were persecuted under the Penal Laws, and forbidden to practise their religion, the people gathered secretly in caves at Portrane, County Dublin to celebrate mass. Fresh water fills the well within the caves and although sea water surrounds it at high tide, the water in the well remains fresh. Chink Well gets its name from the cure that it is associated with, where it was believed to cure chin cough (the old name for whooping cough). Pieces of bread were left as offerings, but the cure would only be successful if the offering was left before sunrise and if the next high tide floated the bread out to sea.

St Colman's Well in Salterstown, County Louth, is another well situated right on the sea's waterline which gets hit by waves and filled with sand and shell deposits, yet its water remains fresh. The people traditionally visited this well for eye and malaria cures.

St Colman's Well in Salterstown, County Louth

Bullaun Stone at St Lasair's Well in Kilronan, County Roscommon. The water that gathered in the hole of a bullaun stone, often found near holy wells, was also believed to have curative properties and to protect against illness and evil (for example, by applying it to a wart or other afflicted area).

It wasn't just water gathered from sacred sites that was believed to have power. Dew was gathered into a bottle before dawn during the month of May and was most powerful if gathered on the first day of May, known as May Day. It was collected either from grass or wrung from cloths left out, and then used for immunity against freckles or wrinkles, or as a cure for headaches, sore skin or eyes. Walking in dew was believed to cure sore feet including bunions or corns. Similarly, the first water scooped from the home's domestic well on May Day was believed to have the power to cure (or in the wrong hands, to curse) the family, so was fiercely protected that morning to ensure only the family had access to their well.

Holy wells are still regarded as sacred places, with many offerings still left at these sites by pilgrims hoping for cures to their present-day ailments.

TREES

Alongside water and stones, trees are the third important component of most sacred sites across Ireland, with whitethorn and ash being the most common. People would take home a leaf or twig from a sacred tree to protect their house from fires for that year, and so common was this practice that a tree at St Moling's Well had to be fenced off to allow it to regenerate. If a holy well was dry in the summer, taking a part of the tree would make a good substitute for the water. Sacred trees are believed to be impossible to burn (similar to the water of a holy well being impossible to boil) and should never be used for firewood.

A rag tree at St Patrick's Chair and Well, Altadaven, County Tyrone, with personal items left on and around the tree as offerings to seek a blessing or a cure. Steps on the right lead up to St Patrick's Chair.

Kilkeasy Graveyard, County Kilkenny, where people would lower small containers tied to a string into the hole in this tree to collect the water that accumulated within the trunk. They would then drink it or bring it home in little bottles, as there was a firm belief that it would cure toothache and warts. There is a story that a man let an eggcup fall into the tree when doing this, but was not able to get it back up again. It's therefore likely that this tree has similarly retained other objects over its long life.

Offerings can be seen even today tied to these trees at holy wells. Traditionally, rags were dipped in the water, used to wash the afflicted body part and then hung on the tree. If a person were bedbound, a piece from their bedclothes would be dipped into the well and tied to the tree. As the rags were traditionally made from natural fibres, they would rot away on the tree, and as the object disintegrated, so too the illness was believed to fade away. The rags used were commonly red, a colour believed to resist evil spirits. The people at that time would therefore wear red flannel over a troubled body part to cure it; for example, wearing a red flannel vest was thought to cure a chest infection.

Ireland has a long history of revering our native trees. Sacred trees were referred to as *bile* in our ancient texts and associated with inauguration sites of the kings of Ireland, where rivals targeted each other's sacred *bile*. In ancient times, the druids favoured the wood of the yew, hawthorn and rowan for their wands and they ate acorns to prepare themselves for prophecy. So important were trees that many of the symbols that created our ancient Irish alphabet, Ogham, are based on the names of our trees. In later texts, mainly written between the seventh and ninth centuries, that record the laws of the old Gaelic legal system (Brehon Law), the importance of trees is clear, as harm to trees was punishable on a scale of severity depending on the damage and type of tree (including its economic value).

One of the most valuable trees under Brehon Law, called 'lords of the wood', was the hazel, which was valued for its rods and its nuts. These nuts also feature in our mythology: nine special hazel trees dropped their magic hazelnuts into a well and the fish that ate them became the salmon of knowledge that Fionn MacCumhaill ultimately tasted and acquired his powers from. Hazel walking sticks were regarded as blessed, and as protecting their owners from fairies.

Another lord of the wood was the oak, with its acorns that could fatten pigs, its wood singled out to build early Christian churches and its bark used for tanning leather. In folklore, it was believed that a mixture derived from its bark (boiled in water, which resulted in a mixture that smelled like tar) would, when drunk, cure rheumatism, jaundice or sore feet, and a common

An example of how old yew trees can grow: this European yew, which has been standing strong for over 750 years, is one of a few trees that could be the oldest in Ireland. This tree was already almost 300 years old when it witnessed the siege of the nearby Geraldine Castle (in the background of the photograph) in the sixteenth century. The castle's owner, Thomas Fitzgerald, known as Silken Thomas, acting Lord Deputy of Ireland, led a rebellion against King Henry VIII. Silken Thomas played the lute underneath this tree the night before he surrendered, and he was subsequently hanged in London along with his five uncles. It is called the Silken Thomas Yew. Maynooth, County Kildare.

application on the farm was to rub it on a horse's chest to toughen it up against the friction of the collar and cure its sores.

Yet another lord of the wood under Brehon Law was the yew, a tree that is especially long-lived and was used for making domestic vessels. Yew trees were often planted near castles as a source of wood for making longbows (due to its elasticity, strength and light weight). The druids preferred yew over other kinds of wood for making their wands. Most parts of the tree are highly poisonous to humans and animals – one reason why they are planted in church sites is to prevent people grazing their animals there – but a compound in yew has been extracted and developed in modern pharmaceuticals with success in treating some forms of cancer, a cure remarkably similar to local folklore

A spindle tree (top right) on a famine path hidden within a hedgerow. This was a secret route for people to get to mass in Penal times. Cullohill, County Laois.

Spindle fruit, which splits open to reveal orange seeds known as arils

recorded in the 1930s by a schoolchild in County Carlow: 'Mrs Doyle Yew Tree Clonegal cures cancer but keeps secret.'

The spindle fell into a lower division of tree under Brehon Law, and damaging one would incur a fine of a young female cow. Dye or ink could be made from the fruit, and it could be baked and powdered as a cure for scabies and headlice. Its narrow, straight branches, which could be shaved into a point, were ideal for use as knitting needles or making spindles for spinning wool. Today, a spindle tree is an indicator that you might be in an ancient Irish woodland.

Whitethorn, also known as hawthorn or *sceach*, when standing alone (a lone bush or fairy tree) is where fairies were believed to live or to pass by, so to disturb one or cut one down brings bad luck. These fairy trees can often be seen with offerings similar to those at the sacred trees at holy wells, including rags or ribbons tied to the branches, and personal items left inside their trunks. Whitethorn is regarded as a sacred tree and they have been used to mark the spot where a person died during The Great Hunger, or to mark the graves of unbaptised children. Planned roads in Ireland have been diverted around them, so strong is the belief, even today. A cure for warts was to rub a snail (or slug) on the wart and then impale the snail on the thorn of a whitethorn (or blackthorn); the wart would wither away as the snail withered. For May Day, an important celebration to welcome the summer, a 'may bush' was set up outside the house, decorated with eggs or ribbon. The tree used differed in each area, with hawthorn a popular choice in many areas, which was thought to keep away *piseogs* (fairies/bad luck) and protect crops and milk.

Blackthorn rods, with their long, sharp thorns, were woven into the top of field fences, similar to how we would use barbed wire today, and are still commonly found growing on fairy forts, earthen mounds that formed part of prehistoric dwellings (ring forts). It was unlucky to cut blackthorn due to its association with the fairies. Stories about pots of gold being buried under blackthorn trees are common.

Elder, known as the boor tree, was believed to cure toothache (by applying the juice or pushing a leaf or other part of the tree into the tooth). The bark

A whitethorn tree, also known as a lone tree or fairy tree

Blackthorn tree with its spikes and berries, which are called sloe berries and used to make sloe gin

Elder tree, Faughart Old Graveyard, County Louth

was used to cure burns and prevent scarring, and the berries or flowers were used to make a remedy for rheumatism. Elder was believed to be associated with biblical stories. It was thought unlucky to strike a person or animal with an elder (as they would not grow any more) or to burn an elder. Gardeners put elder twigs between cabbage plants to protect against cabbage butterflies laying their eggs – it was thought to be poisonous to caterpillars.

Other trees had curative or magical properties. Rowan, or mountain ash, was used to protect against charms and spells. For example, it would be tied around a butter churn to protect or to help make butter; and, conversely, used as a curse to bring misfortune on a family by tying it to their gate post. The bark of the black sally, willow that grows wild, was used to cure headaches, and children were passed through a hoop made from sally rods as a cure for a hernia. A poultice made from the leaves of the elm reduced swelling and its bark helped heal burns. A fire lit using an ash tree would banish the devil; this is one of the few types of wood that can be used to light a fire without being seasoned.

BLESSED CLAY

There were old beliefs among Irish Catholics that clay, or soil, could sometimes have curative or protective properties, for example clay blessed by a priest or taken from the grave of a special person. Various traditions applied to lifting the clay, such as reciting certain prayers, or returning the soil within a certain number of days for the cure to work.

One such site is the grave of a reputed faith healer, Father James McGirr, who promised that after he died, the clay that covered him would cure anything that he was able to cure in life. Thus when he died in 1803, his grave in Boho Cemetery, County Fermanagh, became a source of healing clay, believed to cure minor ailments including wounds and sore throats. The tradition was to kneel beside the plot, remove a small amount of soil and wrap it in a cotton pouch, and without speaking to anyone, return home and place the pouch under your pillow. The clay had to be returned to the grave on the fourth day.

Modern microbiologists have tested the soil and have found that it has unique antibiotic properties, which they are studying in the fight against antibiotic-resistant bacteria.

In Shanrahan Cemetery, County Tipperary, a little iron door was built into the tomb of Father Nicholas Sheehy so that people could access the clay. Father Sheehy was executed in 1766 on a false murder charge. He had defended his starving congregation against Penal Laws designed to keep them subjugated, and against high rents and the enclosure of common grazing land. He was hanged, and his head was displayed on a pole above Clonmel Gaol for over ten years. His tomb became a place of pilgrimage and its clay was believed to have healing powers.

Some people believed the clay taken from their local graveyard would banish rats when sprinkled around, or improve their crops if placed in the four corners of their field.

Normal soil (not taken from special graves or from a graveyard generally) could also become consecrated by being blessed by a priest, after which it

Spoons for scooping the blessed clay from Father James McGirr's grave at Sacred Heart Church Cemetery, Boho, County Fermanagh

A small door in the tomb of Father Nicholas Sheehy allows access to the clay within. Shanrahan Cemetery, Clogheen, County Tipperary.

was also believed to hold special qualities. The custom of using this soil at funerals may date to Penal times, when priests were under threat of severe punishment or death for performing Catholic rituals, so it was not always possible to have a priest perform a funeral. While hiding from priest catchers, he would secretly bless clay on the morning of a funeral; it would then be put in a little linen bag, transported to the cemetery by another person, and thrown into the grave before the coffin was lowered. In Ballinaglera Parish in Leitrim, each townland kept a kit so that if a priest was not available, a layman could preside over a funeral: consecrated clay, a wooden cross, holy water and some straw was kept in a special oval-shaped wicker basket designed for the purpose.

To deal with the risk to the deceased's soul of burying the corpse in unconsecrated ground, blessed clay could be rubbed on the lips of the

The grave of Father Daniel Kavanagh, St Mullins, County Carlow

deceased or placed in the coffin itself and sprinkled on the top when it was lowered. The Board of Guardians of Wexford Workhouse noted in 1870 that their paupers' graveyard had no record of ever having been consecrated, so the staff had a practice of placing consecrated clay under the heads of the dead in the coffin when they were being taken from the workhouse to be interred there. At St James's in Dublin City, if a Catholic was being buried there when the graveyard was under Protestant control, they would secrete consecrated clay beneath the corpse's head.

There was criticism of the Catholic Church in an anonymous letter (signed 'Hibernicus') to a newspaper in 1843:

> In my native parish I have known the clay after being blessed, (when the poverty of the parties prevented them from paying the fee) to be locked up till they applied to their neighbours & made a collection among them, or pledged some article to raise the amount demanded by the charitable Priest.

St Lasair's Holy Well. The clay taken from near the original well (which dried up and moved) was believed to be so powerful that an emigrant sailing to America used it to calm a storm. St Lasair is said to have blessed the clay to cure a soldier of his wounds. Kilronan, County Roscommon.

Special clay could also be taken from a holy well, either lifted along with the water or, if the well was dry, instead of the water. In St Mullin's, County Carlow, the belief was that a person suffering from toothache could be cured if they took clay from the grave of a Catholic priest, Father Daniel Kavanagh (replacing it with clay from elsewhere) and put it in their mouth, together with water from the nearby St Moling's holy well. Similarly, the water from St Seachnall's Well in Dunshaughlin, County Meath, and clay taken from an adjacent stream was mixed and the paste applied to a swelling on the body

This grave slab is cut away to allow access to the soil of Father McGovern's grave, which is taken with spoons while saying certain prayers, and must be returned within three days. In the 1930s, an old man claimed that when he was a young boy back in the nineteenth century, his parents put this blessed clay on his swollen, painful knee and at twelve o'clock that night he felt five cold fingers nibbling down his knee. The bandages were removed and his knee was fully cured. Creevelea Friary, County Leitrim.

Inside a sweathouse, which had corbelled or lintelled roofs with an adjustable opening to control draught for the fire

Jane Doherty was a huge girl that lived in that part. She went one Sunday to the sweat house and some of the good boys stole her clothes and poor Jane had to go home naked. This girl was one of the last to use it. She was a famous girl in her day. Stood to six foot high and was built in proportion. Not a man round the place was able to wrestle her. She challenged Robert Quale's father to wrestle her. The parson used to go down to Quales's and he was afraid of her. Robert Hamilton of Drumshanbo today went to court her and he was not able to get his arms around her. Jane went to America.

One of the earliest written records of a sweathouse in operation comes from the French traveller De Latocnaye, who toured Ireland in 1796–7, and described how the sweathouse he saw in County Donegal was used to treat rheumatism and other maladies such as sore eyes. He went on to explain how the thimble-shaped 'oven' was heated with turf, exactly as a stone oven would be heated for baking bread. Four or five men or women, entirely naked, crawled in and the entrance was sealed up with a piece of wood covered over with dung. They then had to stay inside for hours and even if one of them took ill, the plank would not be taken away before the proper time. After abundant perspiration, when they came out they were commonly much thinner than when they went in. Then some would lie in bed and keep themselves warm; others would simply put on their clothes and go back to work as if nothing special had happened.

These simple structures haven't attracted an ancient written record, and are difficult to date, so theories abound as to their age. Given their similarity to early Scandinavian saunas, some theories suggest they were brought to Ireland by Viking invaders ('the Danes', as Irish people called them). Yet at the ancient monastic settlement on Inishmurray (an island off the coast of County Sligo), nineteenth-century antiquarian scholars found that there was a tradition that a beehive cell had been used as a sweathouse. The locals were still actually calling it *teach an alais*, meaning sweathouse. Since it matched the rest of the ancient monastic buildings, they believed this indicated that the sweathouse was used as far back as the sixth century AD. In County Fermanagh, charred wood found in one sweathouse was carbon-dated to as far back as the fifth century AD. Given these early dates, sweathouses might even date as far back as our prehistoric ancestors.

With so little known about their history, it has also been asked whether it is possible that Christian monks may have crawled into sweathouses to gain a psychedelic experience after ingesting mushrooms and whether that might have informed the unusual artworks they produced.

Sweathouses generally went out of use in the latter half of the nineteenth century. There has been no one particular reason identified for this, but it's likely that the introduction of modern healthcare and running water had an effect. Most sweathouses now lie cold and collapsed in our fields.

Sweathouse, Killadiskert, County Leitrim

Funeral on Inis Mór, Aran Islands, County Galway. Photograph by Heinrich Becker. (© National Folklore Collection, UCD.)

DEATH

THE WAKE

There were different customs to mark a death, but generally the window was opened to let the soul go out, the clock was stopped to show the time the person died, and the mirror was covered or turned in to the wall (one local explanation for this was, 'if you chanced to see the corpse thro the looking glass first, it meant harm would fall to you'). The body would be laid out on a table or, in some areas, on straw on the floor and ritually washed by the neighbours. The water was carefully disposed of where nobody could walk on it, for example inside the stones of a wall or under a bush. Before the times when the deceased person was brought to the church, they were laid out in the house for the duration of the wake, often in a brown habit and cap, and a canopy was formed with white sheets propped on sally (willow) rods or string, with a sheet lying on the body. A black ribbon might adorn the body of a

A selection of old clay pipes. (On display at Glenview Folk Museum, Ballinamore, County Leitrim.)

married adult, a white ribbon if they were unmarried, and the body of a child might be adorned with flowers.

Visitors arriving would always ask the time of death (checking the stopped clock to get their answer) and would be offered tea – it was thought unlucky not to accept tea at the wake. The same applied to smoking tobacco in a pipe or taking snuff, plenty of which would have been bought with the funeral goods. The snuff (finely ground tobacco leaves) was served on a saucer, often resting on the chest or legs of the corpse, or alongside it on a table with candles. People went over to the corpse, took a pinch of snuff, and offered a prayer such as 'Lord have mercy on him'. People even brought little tin containers to take some away with them too, with snuff from a wake believed in some areas to cure headaches.

The clay pipes (*dúidíní*) were usually a type made especially for wakes, with smaller bowls that required less tobacco and often with longer shanks, and were bought in large quantities of at least twelve dozen (a measurement known as a gross), but often several hundred were bought for a wake. They were circulated, already filled with tobacco, around the room in a skib (a shallow circular wicker basket). On taking one, the same prayer – 'Lord have mercy on him' – would be said, and a folklore record tells how this type of pipe became known as 'a Lord have mercy'. The wake was therefore a smoky affair, since most people would smoke a pipe to accept the hospitality offered and to show their respect. There are several origin stories recorded in folklore accounts as to why pipes were smoked at Irish funerals, which included religious links such as how Mary, the mother of Christ, smoked the first pipe during her son's passion and how the apostles smoked at Jesus' wake and at his grave. There was an idea that tobacco protected the living from the ailment that had carried off the dead person.

Although tobacco had only been introduced to Ireland in the seventeenth century, it had become a firm tradition at wakes in the centuries that followed, up to around the time of the world wars, with some accounts blaming this on the burning down of the main pipe-manufacturing village, Knockcroghery, County Roscommon, by the British administration's Black and Tans in 1921.

Incidentally, tobacco was grown successfully in Ireland over the centuries, becoming quite an industry until it was banned intermittently by various British laws to support British colonies and reap the excise benefits. The most common form of tobacco used in the pipes in Ireland was called 'twist': dampened tobacco leaves twisted into a rope shape, secured at intervals with string, and left to mature. It was then sold by length rather than weight.

The wake could be a mix of sadness and fun, where the mourning mingled with dancing and games. A popular game was called *Thart a' Bhróg*, where the men and boys sat closely together in a circle on the floor with their feet out before them, and one remained in the centre. Straw was twisted into a hard mallet-shaped weapon, around two feet (60 cm) long, or an old shoe might be used. The weapon was used to hit the person in the centre, whose aim was to try to identify who had it and to catch it. It was passed from person to person in the circle, at times hidden under their legs, until it was caught. Then the person it was caught from had to swap places with the centre person.

Wakes were described by the author William O'Regan in 1817 as:

> a theatre on which tragedy, comedy, broad farce, match-making, speech-making, &c. all that is bizarre and comical in the genuine Irish character, develope themselves with a freedom truly fantastic. [...] The transitions from the deepest and most impassioned tones of sorrow, to mirth and humour, are quick as thought. There is a melancholy in their mirth, and a mirth in their melancholy.

THE BURIAL

Burial in many areas took place on the afternoon of the third day after death. The body would be placed in the coffin, after any fastenings had been removed (so the soul could move freely in the otherworld), and a pad of hay, or shavings from the wood used to make the coffin, would be placed under the head. Ready-made coffins weren't available until the beginning of the twentieth century, so the family would buy the boards of wood themselves, along with the funeral provisions, and have the coffin made. For adult burials, the coffin was often black, either painted or with black cloth tacked on it, and for children, white linen was used with a blue ribbon cross.

The mourners carried the body in the coffin out of the house, feet first, and laid it on two chairs outside the door. Then the lid was put on and the coffin was carried from the house to the graveyard at a fast walking pace (four to five miles per hour). The coffin was carried on a bier (or bearer), often two long poles joined together by lathes, or using sheets twisted underneath the coffin.

De Profundis Stone in Kilbride, County Westmeath. Funeral processions gathered to rest the coffin on this stone, carved at least three hundred years ago. The chief mourners would sit on the ledge at the wall and the De Profundis (Psalm 130) would be recited in Latin, the opening line of which is 'Out of the depths I cry to you, O Lord.' The last burial at which the coffin was rested here and the psalm recited was in 1937.

Depending on the importance of the person in the local community, funeral processions could sometimes be huge affairs. At one nineteenth-century funeral there were around two thousand attendees and the procession stretched a mile in length. It was deemed unlucky if a person passing a funeral did not turn back to accompany the funeral, even for a short distance.

A prescribed traditional route was always travelled, with no shortcut allowed. There might be a circuit of the town square where the village cross stood; this tradition continued even when the cross was long gone, as is still the case in Navan, County Meath.

It was the custom in many areas to set the coffin down on the way to the graveyard at funeral halts; special points on the route such as a wayside cross, a particular stone (thus called a coffin stone) or a heap of stones, often located at the crossroads nearest the graveyard. The coffin might also be rested outside

Coffin rest, Kiltullagh, County Galway, which was once a stile in a wall. The coffin was set down here and prayers said, before the mourners passed through it to cross the field to the cemetery behind. A local person informed the author that it is known as The Corpse Gate.

Wooden crosses near St Mary's Cemetery, Kilmore, County Wexford. A wooden cross was made from the wood used to make the coffin and left at the crossroads nearest the cemetery.

the graveyard itself, on the graveyard wall, or in an old ruined church on the site. Generally, there was an aversion in most areas to setting the coffin down directly on the ground.

Special prayers would be said at the coffin rest, such as the De Profundis. This tradition is thought to have originated in Penal times when there was a law against celebrating Catholic ceremonies within a graveyard on the occasion of a burial, so the mourners could not pray at the grave itself. It was the prayers said over the body that were important, not the physical location where they were said.

At the designated coffin rest, there were also traditions of the mourners leaving offerings such as stones or little crosses known as crusheens (or *croisíní*, little crosses) in memory of the dead who passed by on the way to their last resting place. In Wexford, a 1930s account described a custom that had been commonly practised in local villages:

The Heap of Crosses, Ballygrangans, County Wexford, where the tradition continues at the point where the funeral procession used to leave the road to 'wend its sorrowful way' on the traditional route to Grange Cemetery

In all these places the pieces of wood remaining over from the boards out of which the coffin has been made were fashioned into crosses a couple of feet high and painted in various colours. These were then carried by the chief mourners and placed on or at the foot of a hawthorn or ash tree convenient to the cross roads nearest to the graveyard towards which the funeral wends its sorrowful way.

Another account tells how, in addition to leaving a cross at the sacred tree, another wooden cross was made and carried by the mourners to be placed at the head of the grave in the cemetery. Similar traditions were found in

Crosses left by passing funerals at the Joyce memorial in Cong, County Mayo. The plaque is inscribed 'Pray for the soules of John Joyce and Mary Joyce his wife who dyed 6th August, 1712.' They had resisted a neighbouring family who came to abduct their daughter for a forced marriage. Three young men, brothers, were later hanged at Ballinrobe Gaol for their involvement. The practice of leaving small crosses at certain locations in Cong is said to date to 1542, with the three locations called The Cresheens. Up until then, the canons had brought the processional Cross of Cong to a certain point in the road to meet incoming funerals, but when the abbey was suppressed and the banished monks were leaving their abbey, they met a funeral and the Lord Abbot instead formed a cross from branches of a tree, which he placed on the roadside, said a prayer for the dead, and added 'Thus let it be done for all time.'

Stone crosses at a crossroads in Carrig-on-Bannow, County Wexford, with wooden crosses placed behind. The artist's caption was 'Resting Place for Funerals'. Sketched by W. Frazer (d. 1905), as copied from an earlier work by G. Du Noyer (d. 1869). (© National Library of Ireland.)

The stone crosses at Carrig-on-Bannow, County Wexford, where the local custom was for the mourners on a funeral procession to leave a wooden cross

County Mayo and in France, which, along with County Wexford, were areas associated with St Fursey in the seventh century and also with Cistercian and Augustinian Christian orders (which came from France in the twelfth century), so there are theories linking these locations to this tradition.

A practical reason for these traditions was to rest the coffin bearers and allow them to swap with another group of men, but may go beyond simply resting the coffin, as some stones are recorded as associated with honour, such as the stone in County Clare known as Cloch na h-Onóra (the 'stone of honour').

Within the graveyard, taking the coffin to the grave had its own customs too. The coffin might be brought along by the boundary wall 'east to west by the south' a certain number of times, depending on the local tradition, or it might be touched down to a special stone or piece of blessed earth (such as at Fenloe Graveyard in County Clare), and then approach the grave.

Coffin rest built into the graveyard wall in Fenagh Abbey, County Leitrim, the design of which made it easier to pass the coffin over the wall

The skib filled with pipes would be brought to the graveyard and the pipes smoked again in honour of the deceased, with an expression such as 'God be merciful to the soul of him that this pipe was over', with the custom often including leaving the pipe on the grave or burying it in the topsoil.

The nails or screws of the lid would be removed to allow the deceased person's soul get to the otherworld; sod or straw was placed on the coffin to muffle the thud of earth being shovelled on it; and the mourners only left when the spade and shovel were crossed over the closed grave.

Salruck Graveyard, Little Killary, County Galway, where clay pipes were left directly on the graves. In 1905, the local priest ordered the pipes away, after which they were placed into containers (© National Library of Ireland).

Salruck Graveyard, Little Killary, County Galway. The tradition of leaving clay pipes is no longer visible. Graves here were traditionally marked with a bed of stones.

KEENING

There are written records going back to the sixteenth century about keening (from the Irish *caoine*, meaning mourn or to cry), which was singing a lament over the dead, such as '*ochón, ochón eile, ullulu*'. Many believed this helped the soul to leave the body. This could be performed by the family and mourners, but some women were especially skilled as keeners and would be paid to do so (including with glasses of whiskey). There was opposition to keening from the authorities, including from the Protestant and Catholic Churches, who regarded it as barbarous and inappropriate. The corporations of Kilkenny and Galway banned it outright in 1609 and 1626 respectively, on pain of a fine, although this threat did not succeed in preventing it.

A funeral procession in Connemara, County Galway, in a sketch printed in 1870, with women keening, one throwing her hands up with her lament. Note the bier (coffin bearer) on a cart under the coffin.

A French visitor to Ireland in 1797 witnessed keening, describing the women chanting what sounded to his foreign ear like 'hu lu hi', which he thought resembled a chant of the De Profundis, beating their breasts, weeping freely, tearing their hair, and throwing themselves down on the coffin bier. He particularly noted a difference between regions; he saw no keening when he visited the northern counties. Other visitors in earlier centuries reported similar scenes and described the sound of keening as 'sometimes so violent as though they were distracted, sometimes as it were in a kind of singing', where 'they spread their palms, they raise their hands to the heavens, they shake the coffin ...'. The *Dublin Penny Journal* in 1833 described the sound as unearthly, guttural and plaintive, swelling and softening, the deeper tones of the men's voices joining in at certain points.

By the early twentieth century, only the oldest people remembered having heard it in childhood.

UNDERTAKERS

While most of the funeral arrangements were made by the family and supported by friends and neighbours, funeral directors (known as undertakers) also had a role. Pubs and undertakers often fell under the same ownership in villages and towns throughout Ireland.

Coffins being stored at the back of McCarthy's pub in Fethard, County Tipperary

McCarthy's, Fethard, County Tipperary, which offers an undertaking service to this day

The origin of this was the time of the Great Hunger. To cope with the volume of deaths in communities and to store the bodies in a cool place until the coroner arrived, the Coroners (Ireland) Act, 1846 mandated that the corpse be brought to the nearest public house (the place most likely to have a cellar, and one of the only community spaces at the time), with a fine incurred if they refused. The coroner would then travel to the area and the inquest(s) would take place in the pub itself. Publicans naturally widened their services to support wakes and other funeral arrangements. There are pubs associated with funeral services even to this day.

Frank Mannion Lounge Bar, Undertaker & Funeral Home, Abbeyknockmoy, County Galway

MEMORIALS

When people were killed or found dead on the roadside (for example during the Great Hunger or during plagues), the site would be marked in some way by a memorial monument (*leacht cuimhne* in Irish), even though the body would likely be buried elsewhere. A cross might be erected, a tree planted, or a heap of stones created (known as a cairn, or *carn* in Irish), and people who passed by would add a pebble or a stone to the 'melancholy memorial' and say a prayer to honour and remember the person who died there. This was also believed

Roadside death cairn near Ros Dumhach (Rossport), County Mayo (© National Folklore Collection, UCD)

The Sailor's Grave, a memorial cairn on the coast at Balbriggan, County Dublin, where fifteen men died when their ship, Bell Hill, *careered into the reef in a gale in 1875. This spot is possibly where their bodies lay after being pulled from the sea, as local custom in many counties was to build cairns where dead bodies touched the ground. Local people continue to follow the ancient tradition of adding a stone as they pass by, in memory of these men and also in memory of all those who have lost their lives off this coast.*

to help them in the otherworld, although in a small number of cases it was to ward off the ghost of the person who died.

It is thought this tradition stretches back to prehistory; similar cairns were built on the tops of mountains for chieftains and kings. Many roadside cairns were removed in times past when roads were improved, but there was great superstition around this, with illness or bad luck believed to befall those who removed them.

A memorial to Thomas Healy, lying under an oak tree at Kyleva, County Kilkenny, who died at the roadside on 10 November 1840. This corner is known as 'the Monuments' and includes several other memorial structures. An old whitethorn tree previously grew here.

If a lone tree, usually a whitethorn (hawthorn), was planted where somebody died or a heap of stones or other marker recorded the site of a death, they were known locally as a monument tree or a monument. Thus, Irish people remembered their dead at these sites even when carrying out their daily activities.

Two of the three memorial cairns at the Monuments, Kyleva, County Kilkenny. The antiquarian Richard Hitchcock observed in 1852 that Kyleva Monuments was 'several small carn-like monuments, at the road side … These little monuments are remarkable, as having been raised to the memories of persons who, I was told, had died and were buried elsewhere, and one or two have young trees growing on them.' A local man remembers his father telling him in the 1950s that funeral processions would rest coffins on the cairns to allow the coffin carriers to change over and that there may originally have been five cairns. He recalls that the three cairns had the appearance of a dry stone wall construction – although similarly flat-topped and columnar – but that they were cemented by the Board of Works in the 1980s.

*Young man making a crios, a traditional woven belt,
County Galway. (© National Folklore Collection, UCD.)*

AFTERWORD

The remnants documented in this book tell the story of the many generations of Irish people who have gone before us, their beliefs and traditions and the constant challenges they faced. Their survival depended on their skills and craftsmanship, their connection with the land and sea, and the support they gave to each other as a community, which in turn made them the people that they were.

In the late nineteenth/early twentieth century, the playwright and writer John Millington Synge stayed with islanders on the remote Aran Islands, untouched by modernisation at that time. He observed the men, women and children working together and how the character of the people was directly influenced by the activities in their daily lives, many of which have left traces in our landscape:

> It is likely that much of the intelligence and charm of these people is due to the absence of any division of labour, and to the correspondingly wide development of each individual, whose varied knowledge and skill necessitates a considerable activity of mind. Each man can speak two languages. He is a skilled fisherman, and can manage a curagh with extraordinary nerve and dexterity. He can farm simply, burn kelp, cut out pampooties [rawhide shoes], mend nets, build and thatch a house, and make a cradle or a coffin. His work changes with the seasons in a way that keeps him free from the dullness that comes to people who have always the same occupation. The danger of his life on the sea gives him the alertness of a primitive hunter, and the long nights he spends fishing in his curagh bring him some of the emotions that are thought peculiar to men who have lived with the arts.

Many of the objects and ruins featured in this book continue to slowly decay, but through them and through our knowledge of their stories we can nurture our connection to the people whose lives they touched. We continue to remember those who came before us through these remnants of our past.

BIBLIOGRAPHY

THE HOUSEHOLD
Food and Drink

Clancy, E. & Forde Patrick J., 1980, *Ballinaglera Parish, Co. Leitrim: Aspects of Its History and Traditions*, p. 42.

Connell, K. H., 1965, 'The Potato in Ireland', *Clogher Record*, 5(3), pp. 281–295.

Danaher, Kevin, 1962, *In Ireland Long Ago*, pp. 37–57.

Danaher, Kevin, 2023 (first published 1972), *The Year in Ireland: Irish Calendar Customs*.

De Latocnaye, Chevalier, 1797 (translated by John Stevenson, 1917), *A Frenchman's Walk through Ireland*, pp.76, 92.

'Dublin Markets', *The Leinster Express*, 13/02/1847.

'Glimpses of the Past from the Dublin Newspapers of 1787', *Dublin Penny Journal*, 21/03/1903, p. 616.

Evans, E. Estyn, 1957 (reissued 2000), *Irish Folk Ways*, pp. 61, 219.

'Hibernian Bakery,' *The Cork Examiner*, 29/05/1844.

Johnson, Dr J., 1844, *A Tour in Ireland with Meditations and Reflections*, pp. 313–314.

Joyce, P. W., 1910, *English As We Speak It In Ireland*, 'Dip', p. 247.

Keating, Geoffrey, 1634 (translated by John O'Mahony, 1857), *The History of Ireland from the earliest period to the English invasion*.

Kerrigan, Agnes (Mayo County Council), 2006, Fulacht Fiadh, Cashelduff IV, Co. Mayo.

Lawless, Christy, 1990, 'A Fulacht Fiadh Bronze Age Cooking Experiment at Turlough, Castlebar', *Cathair na Mart:Journal of the Westport Historical Society*, 10(1), pp.1–10.

Miller, I., 2022, 'Tea Mania', *History Ireland*, 30 (2).

Mulcahy, John. D., 2022, 'Relish, Condiment, Kitchen: Bastions of Irish Food Practice for Fourteen Hundred Years'.

O'Brien, William, 2012, 'Aspects of fulacht fiadh function and chronology in Cork', *Journal of The Cork Historical and Archaeological Society*, 117, pp.107–133.

O'Cleirigh, Nellie, 1992, *Valentia: A Different Irish Island*, p. 85.

Ó'Riordáin, Seán, 1942 (revised reprint 1984), *Antiquities of the Irish Countryside*, pp. 84–88.

'Potatoes with the Bones in', *The Cork Examiner*, '03/06/1844.

The National Folklore Collection, University College Dublin, The Main Manuscript Collection.

The National Folklore Collection, University College Dublin, The Schools' Collection.

Tobin, Richard, 2022, 'Nineteenth-Century Bread Ovens of the Blackwater Valley in County Waterford', *European Journal of Food Drink and Society*, 2(1), Article 4.

Tully Cross Guild Irish Countrywomen's Association, 1985, *Portrait of a Parish: Ballynakill, Connemara*, p. 104.

Wilde, W., 1854, 'Food of the Irish', *Dublin University Magazine.*

Washing Day

Carty, Mary-Rose, 1991, *History of Killeen Castle.*

Fleming, Maurice, 2002, *Not of this World: creatures of the supernatural in Scotland*, pp. 3–5.

Hinkson, Pamela (as told to), 1937 (reprinted 2009), *Seventy Years Young, Memories of Elizabeth, Countess of Fingall*, pp. 102–103.

Joyce, P. W., 1910, 'Banshee', *English As We Speak It In Ireland*, p. 214.

Mooney, James, 1888, *The Funeral Customs of Ireland*, p. 261.

Moore M. B. & Beryl F. E., 'Mary Anne Cruise of Rathmore & Cruicetown', navanhistory.ie.

Rankine, David, 2005, *The Guises of the Morrigan: the Irish Goddess of Sex and Battle, her myths, powers and mysteries*, p. 26.

Schoepperle, G., 1919, 'The Washer of the Ford', *The Journal of English and Germanic Philology*, 18(1), pp. 60–66.

Thackeray, W.M., 1843, *The Irish Sketch Book*, p.172.

The National Folklore Collection, University College Dublin, The Main Manuscript Collection

The National Folklore Collection, University College Dublin, The Schools' Collection

NFCS, 0527, 063, Mrs. Foley, Clounanna, Co. Limerick.

NFC, 0630, 162.

THE VILLAGE
The Forge

Archer, Patrick, 'Páid O'Donoghue' (poem)

British Houses of Commons Sessional Papers, 1843, Blacksmiths (Ireland), 'A Return from the Clerk of the Peace of Every County in Ireland, of the names and places of abode of every Blacksmith whose forge has been registered, and who has received a Licence at quarter session, during the last 10 years', L, p. 51

UK Parliament, minutes of the British House of Commons debate on the Arms (Ireland) Bill, 29/05/1843, hansard. parliament.uk

Byrne, Miles, 1907, *Memoirs of Miles Byrne (A new edition)*, 1, p. 21.

Clancy, E. & Forde Patrick J., 1980, *Ballinaglera Parish, Co. Leitrim: Aspects of Its History and Traditions*, p. 125.

Danaher, Kevin, 1964, *In Ireland Long Ago*, pp.134–139.

Danaher, Kevin, 2023 (first published 1972), *The Year in Ireland: Irish Calendar Customs*, p. 42.

Department of Housing, Local Government and Heritage, National Monuments Service, Metalworking Site: Druminalass, Historic Environment Viewer.

Doyle, Eamonn, 2008, *Tales of the Anvil: The Forges and Blacksmiths of Wexford.*

'Hammond's Forge Coppenagh' (information plaque at site).

Hogg, William E., 2008, *Smithies of Ireland of the 19th Century.*

Ó Danachair, C., 1963, 'The Spade in Ireland', *Béaloideas*, 31, pp.98–114.

PROI Wood 2/15/25, 'Blacksmiths' Licence Papers and Registers, 1798–1842', accessed on Virtual Records Treasury of Ireland.

Taplin, William, 1793, *The Gentleman's Stable Directory; or, Modern System of Farriery* (twelfth edition).

Thackeray, W.M., 1869, *The Irish Sketch Book*, p. 296.

The National Folklore Collection, University College Dublin, The Main Manuscript Collection.

The National Folklore Collection, University College Dublin, The Schools' Collection.

Tully Cross Guild Irish Countrywomen's Association, 1985, *Portrait of a Parish: Ballynakill, Connemara*, pp.125–126.

Wicklow Gaol (information signs at site).

Horses

Bell, Jonathan & Watson, Mervyn, 2015, 'Bardog Creel', Fermanagh County Museum, fermanaghastoryin100objects.wordpress.com.

Canal & River Trust, 'Rope Marks on Bridges, Nine unusual things for children to spot by the water this summer', canalrivertrust.org.uk.

Canals of Dublin, Granard Bridge, canalsofdublin.com.

Evans, E. Estyn, 1957 (republished 2000), *Irish Folk Ways*, pp.61, 203, 219.

London Canal Museum, Rope Grooves, canalmuseum.org.uk.

O'Connell, Derry, 1975, *The Antique Pavement*.

O'Dowd, Peadar, 2019, 'Galway City's Jostle Stones – Unique Reminders of the Horse-Drawn Transport Era', *Journal of the Galway Archaeological and Historical Society*, 71, pp.134–144.

Sugan Information, Museums of Mayo, museumsofmayo.com.

The National Folklore Collection, University College Dublin, The Main Manuscript Collection.

The National Folklore Collection, University College Dublin, The Photographic Collection.

NFCS, 0952, 152, A.F.M. McAdoo, Nart, Co. Monaghan.

'Wood Paving', 1895, *The British Medical Journal*, 2(1807), p. 439.

Bridges

'Clapper Bridge' (Sonia Kelly), *The Mayo News*, 26/05/2004.

Department of Housing, Local Government and Heritage, National Monuments Service, Clapper Bridge, Graiguenamanagh (Tunney, Mary), Historic Environment Viewer.

Encyclopædia Britannica, 'Clapper Bridge'.

National Monuments Service, Archaeological Survey, Garroman Bridge, County Galway.

O'Sullivan, M. & Downey, L., 2015, 'Historical Bridges', *Archaeology Ireland*, 29(4), pp.37–40.

'Ros a'Locha – An Caol-Átha: Ros O Locha – Clapper Bridge', 2024 (information sign at site).

'The Colony and the Louisburgh Clapper Bridge' (John Healy), *The Mayo News*, 28/06/2016.

The Heritage Council (Cork County Council Heritage Unit), 2013, 'Heritage Bridges of County Cork'.
The National Folklore Collection, University College Dublin, The Schools' Collection.
The Stepping Stones: Clapper-Bridge, 2024 (information sign at site).

The Pound

'Belmullet Petty Sessions, Assault', *The Mayo Examiner*, 06/03/1871.
'Castlebar Petty Sessions', *The Telegraph; or Connaught Ranger*, Assault and Trespass, Michael and Ellen Lavelle v. Margaret Davidson and Hana Carson, 15/05/1844.
'Castlebar Petty Sessions', *The Telegraph; or Connaught Ranger*, 27/02/1856.
Castleisland District Heritage, The Pound, Castleisland: A survey of the era, odonohoearchive.com.
St. Hugh's N.S., 2019, *Fire on the Mountain: Ballinaglera parish in the archives*, 'Clever Police Cattle Raid in Ireland', excerpt from *The Daily East Anglian Times*, 28/10/1909
'County Cork Assizes', *The Kerry Evening Post*, 29/03/1845.
'Mr. Crotty's Claim', *The Mayo Examiner*, 31/07/1871.
'Nenagh Petty Sessions', *The Nenagh Guardian*, 08/12/1852.
'Nenagh Quarter Sessions', *The Nenagh Guardian*, 12/10/1892.
'Provincial Intelligence, Tithes', *The Freeman's Journal*, 17/11/1835.
'Riot and Rescue on the White Mountain', *The Cork Examiner*, 01/06/1842.
'Sensational Seizure of a Hen', *Leinster Leader*, 20/08/1898.
'State of the Country', *The Nenagh Guardian*, 28/08/1839.
'Stradbally Petty Sessions, Trespass', *The Nationalist and Leinster Times*, 19/03/1898.
Summary Jurisdiction (Ireland) Act, 1851.
'Summer Assizes, County Mayo', *The Freeman's Journal*, 10/07/1869.
'Milltown Petty Sessions', *The Kerry Evening Post*, 14/05/1873.
'To the Editor', *The Kerry Sentinel*, 02/05/1891.
The National Folklore Collection, University College Dublin, The Schools' Collection.
'Magisterial Investigation', *The Tuam Herald*, 02/06/1860.
'Report of the Irish Tithe Committee', *The Western Herald*, 21/02/1832.
'Trespass and Poundage (Letter to the Editor)', *The Ballinrobe Chronicle*, 02/11/1867.

THE SEA

Fishing

'Another Terrible Disaster at Valentia, Six Men Drowned', *The Kerry Sentinel*, 19/09/1908.
'Bantry Drowning Tragedy is Remembered', *The Southern Star* (Jackie Keogh), 2018, 01/10/2018.
Blake, John A., 1863, *The Salmon Fisheries of Ireland: Replies to Arguments Advanced against Mr. McMahon's Fishery Bill*.
Danaher, Kevin, 2023 (first published 1972), *The Year in Ireland: Irish Calendar Customs*, p. 14.
De Bovet, Marie Anne, 1891, *Three Months' Tour in Ireland*, pp. 67, 229, 232.

Department of Housing, Local Government and Heritage, National Monuments Service, Fish Palace: Baltimore, CO150-049, Historic Environment Viewer.

Doherty, A., 2020, *Waterford Harbour, Tides and Tales*, pp.44-48.

Dunn, S. & Meide, C., 2014, 'The "Wretched Poor" and the Sea: Contest and exploitation of Achill Island's historic maritime landscape', Human Exploitation of Aquatic Landscapes special issue (ed. Ricardo Fernandes and John Meadows), *Internet Archaeology*.

Dwyer, Fin, 2024, 'Why Didn't Irish People Eat Fish During the Great Hunger?', Irish History Podcast.

Evans, E. Estyn, 1961, *Irish Folk Ways*, pp. 227-229, 233-252.

Foras Na Mara (Marine Institute), Interactive Marine Archive, marine.ie.

Foster, Thomas Campbell, 1846, *Letters on the Condition of the People of Ireland*.

Lane, P. G., 2010, 'Galway and Mayo Fisheries in the Mid Nineteenth Century: Transferable Assets', *Journal of the Galway Archaeological and Historical Society*, 62, pp. 144-156.

O'Cleirigh, Nellie, 1992, *Valentia: A Different Irish Island*, pp.75, 78-79, 99.

O'Flaherty, Liam, 1929, 'The Stone', *The Mountain Tavern and Other Stories*, p. 236.

Roney, John B., 2019, '[Mis-]managing Fisheries on the West Coast of Ireland in the Nineteenth Century', Department of History, Sacred Heart University.

Rynne, Colin, 2015, *Industrial Ireland: An Archaeology*, The Collins Press, pp. 199-204.

Sisk, Honor, 1990, 'The Outer Islands of Clew Bay' *Cathair na Mart: Journal of the Westport Historical Society*, 10(1), pp. 11-38.

Smylie, Mike, 2014, *Ireland: The Fishing Industry Through Time*.

Stagles, Joan and Ray, 1980, *The Blasket Islands: Next Parish America*, p. 67.

Synge, John M., 1912, *The Aran Islands, Part III and IV*, pp. 13, 42.

'The New Ross Fishermen', *The Freeman's Journal*, 26/07/1847.

The National Folklore Collection, University College Dublin, The Main Manuscript Collection.

The National Folklore Collection, University College Dublin, The Schools' Collection.

Tides & Tales: A Maritime Community Project, tidesandtales.ie.

Tully Cross Guild Irish Countrywomen's Association, 1985, *Portrait of a Parish: Ballynakill, Connemara*.

Went, A. E. J., 1955, 'A Short History of the Fisheries of the River Nore', *The Journal of the Royal Society of Antiquaries of Ireland*, 85(1).

Went, A. E. J., 1946, 'Pilchards in the South of Ireland', *Journal of the Cork Historical and Archaeological Society*, 51(174), pp. 137-157.

Wood, Walter, 1911, *North Sea Fishers & Fighters*, p. 123.

Young, Todd. 1975, 'The Dingle Commercial Fishermen: An Analysis of the Economic Action of an Irish Fishing Fleet' Ph.D. dissertation, University of Pittsburgh.

Seaweed

'1852 Agreement Quoted in Seaweed Case', *The Western People*, 09/02/1983.

'Court of Chancery Appeal', *The Freeman's Journal*, 21/11/1874.

'Cutting Seaweed', *The Western People*, 26/08/1910.

'Deplorable Occurrence', *The Kerry Examiner*, 06/07/1849.

Dunn, S. & Meide, C., 2014, 'The "Wretched Poor" and the Sea: Contest and exploitation of Achill Island's historic maritime landscape', Human Exploitation of Aquatic Landscapes special issue (ed. Ricardo Fernandes and John Meadows), *Internet Archaeology*.

Evans, E. Estyn, 1957 (republished 2000), *Irish Folk Ways*, p. 218–232.

Forsythe, W., 2006, *The Archaeology of the Kelp Industry in the Northern Islands of Ireland*.

Glens of Antrim Historical Society, 2014, 'Kelp Burning in the Glens of Antrim by Douglas Harper', antrimhistory.net.

Grant, Kevin, 2019, 'Oran an Fheamnaidh – Song of the Seaweed Gathered: An Archaeology of early 19th-century Kelping', *Scottish Archaeological Journal* 41, pp. 63–85.

'James Hayes v. James Hayes', *Southern Star*, 08/05/1897.

'Kerry Spring Assizes', *The Kerry Evening Post*, 18/03/1863.

Knight, Jasper (ed.), 2002, *Field Guide to the Coastal Environments of Northern Ireland*.

'Melancholy Accident – Seven Lives Lost', *The Kerry Evening Post*, 26/05/1849.

'Melancholy Accident by Drowning', *The Cork Examiner*, 26/05/1849.

National Museum of Ireland, 2021, 'A Brief History of the Kelp Industry in Fanad', ouririshheritage.org.

O'Cleirigh, Nellie, 1992, *Valentia: A Different Irish Island*, p. 96.

O'Flaherty, Liam, 1929, *The Mountain Tavern and Other Stories*, 'The Stone', p. 236.

Service of a Rockite Notice on the Police at Ballylongford', *The Kerry Evening Post*, 01/02/1845.

Stagles, Joan and Ray, 1980, *The Blasket Islands: Next Parish America*, p. 67.

Synge, John M., 1912, *The Aran Islands, Parts I and II*, pp.48-49, *Parts III and IV*, pp. 10–11.

'Seaweed', *The Kerry Evening Post*, 19/04/1845.

The National Folklore Collection, University College Dublin, The Schools' Collection.

Waldron, Michael, and Power, Orla Peach, 'Fisheries and Aquaculture: Seaweed/ Algae Mariculture on Deep Maps Cork', deepmapscork.wordpress.com.

'When Ireland Was Free' – In Erris – Carting Seaweed', *The Ballina Herald*, 02/06/1928.

'Who "Owns" The Sea-Bed?', *The Kerry Sentinel*, 13/03/1888.

Salt

Department of Housing, Local Government and Heritage, National Monuments Service, Historic Environment Viewer.

Forsythe, W., McConkey, R., & Breen, C., 2018, 'Persistence and risk: salt production in post-medieval Ireland', *World Archaeology*, 50(4), pp. 603–619.

Nicholson, C. A., 2014, 'Salt Mines in the Carrickfergus Area of County Antrim', *Journal of the Mining Heritage Trust of Ireland*, 14, pp. 1-22.

O'Sullivan, Muiris, and Downey, Liam, 'Salt-Making and Food Preservation', 2016, *Archaeology Ireland*, 30(4).

Rynne, Colin, 2015, *Industrial Ireland: An Archaeology*, pp. 159, 301-302.

The National Folklore Collection, University College Dublin, The Main Manuscript Collection.

The National Folklore Collection, University College Dublin, C031.24.00001, Kiln under natural rock The National Folklore Collection, University College Dublin, The Schools' Collection.

University of Ulster, Centre for Maritime Archaeology, 2015, 'Carrickfergus and the Discovery of Irish Rock Salt', saltarch.wordpress.com

University of Ulster, Centre for Maritime Archaeology, 2015, The Archaeology of Salt Production in Ireland, 'Ballycastle Salt Pans excavation', saltarch.wordpress.com.

University of Ulster, Centre for Maritime Archaeology, 2015, The Archaeology of Salt Production in Ireland, "'The 'Devil's Churn" at Ballycastle salt works', saltarch.wordpress.com.

THE LAND
Cattle/Rundale/Travelling Labourers/Reliance on Potatoes

Aalen, F.H.A., Whelan, K. & Stout, M., 2011, *Atlas of the Irish Rural Landscape* (second edition).

Asenath Nicholson, 1847, *Ireland's Welcome to the Stranger; or An excursion through Ireland, in 1844 & 1845, for the purpose of personally investigating the condition of the poor*, pp. 135-136, 399-400.

Bartlett, Thomas, 2010, *Ireland, A History*, pp. 139, 164, 166, 199-201, 240, 267, 270-1.

Clancy, E. & Forde Patrick J., 1980, *Ballinaglera Parish, Co. Leitrim: Aspects of Its History and Traditions*, pp. 45, 55-56, 104-105, 111-112.

Costello, Eugene, 2020, *Transhumance and the Making of Ireland's Uplands 1550-1900*.

Danaher, Kevin, 1962, *Gentle Places and Simple Things*, pp. 11, 26.

Danaher, Kevin, 1962, *In Ireland Long Ago*.

Danaher, Kevin, 2023 (first published 1972), *The Year in Ireland: Irish Calendar Customs*, pp. 96, 145-146.

Dunn, S. & Meide, C., 2014, 'The "Wretched Poor" and the Sea: Contest and exploitation of Achill Island's historic maritime landscape', Human Exploitation of Aquatic Landscapes special issue (ed. Ricardo Fernandes and John Meadows), *Internet Archaeology*.

Evans, E. Estyn, 1957 (republished 2000), *Irish Folk Ways* pp. 27-38, 152, 211.

'Achill in Sorrow', *Evening Herald*, 18/06/1894.

Evening Herald, 02/07/1894.

'Fatal Affray in Ireland', *Pictorial Times*, V(122), 12/07/1845.

Flaherty, E., 2015, 'Rundale and 19th Century Irish Settlement: System, Space and Genealogy', *Irish Geography*, 48(2), 3-38.

Keating, John, 1996, *Irish Famine Facts*.

Magan, Manchán, interview with Gerard Mangan, 2021, 'The Deserted Village', The Almanac of Ireland (podcast).

McDonald, Theresa, 1998, 'The Deserted Village, Slievemore, Achill Island, County Mayo, Ireland', *International Journal of Historical Archaeology*, 2(2).

St. Hugh's N.S., 2019, *Fire on the Mountain: Ballinaglera Parish in the archives,* 'West Breffni Reminiscences: Excerpts from the memoir of Anthony Mulvey', pp. 249-260.

National Museum of Ireland, Irish Emigration to America – The Journey, museum.ie.

O'Cleirigh, Nellie, 1992, *Valentia: A Different Irish Island* p. 95.

Ó Danachair, C., 1963, 'The Spade in Ireland', *Béaloideas*, 31, pp. 98-114.

Ó 'Riordáin, Seán, 1942, *Antiquities of the Irish Countryside* (revised reprint 1984), pp. 29-64.

Rynne, Colin, 2015, *Industrial Ireland: An Archaeology.*

Sisk, Honor, 1990, 'The Outer Islands of Clew Bay', *Journal of the Westport Historical Society*, 10(1), pp. 11-38.

Smith, Cynthia E., 1993, 'The Land-Tenure System in Ireland: A Fatal Regime', *Marquette Law Review*, 76(2)

Society of Friends, 1852, *Transactions of the Central Relief Committee during the Famine in Ireland, 1846 and 1847.*

Stagles, Joan and Ray, 1980, *The Blasket Islands, Next Parish America*, pp. 17-18, 79-94.

Synge, John M., 1912, *The Aran Islands, Part I and II*, pp. 1, 33-34, 47.

The Ballinhassig Massacre, *The Freeman's Journal*, 04/07/1845.

'Achill in Sorrow', *Evening Herald*, 18/06/1894.

'The Families of the Victims', *Evening Herald*, 02/07/1894.NFC, T0278.2, J.R., Cornecassa Demesne, Co. Monaghan The National Folklore Collection, University College Dublin, The Schools' Collection.

'The Achill Migrants: The Bothy Fire', *The Western People* , 26/08/1944.

Trench, W, Steuart, 1868, *Realities of Irish Life*, pp. 98-99, 100-103.

Tully Cross Guild Irish Countrywomen's Association, 1985, *Portrait of a Parish: Ballynakill, Connemara*, p. 102.

Lime

Aalen, F.H.A., Whelan, K. & Stout, M., 2011, *Atlas of the Irish Rural Landscape* (second edition), p. 247.

'Accident at a Lime Kiln', *The Nation*, 02/05/1857.

'Burned to Death in a Limekiln', *Evening Herald*, 26/02/1895.

Butler, Jim, 2020, 'Lime Kilns: an overview of the history of lime kilns in Ireland', donardimaalhistory.wicklowheritage.org.

Clancy, E. & Forde Patrick J., 1980, *Ballinaglera Parish, Co. Leitrim: Aspects of Its History and Traditions*, pp. 119-120.

'Death from Falling into Lime Kiln', *The Freeman's Journal*, 10/03/1873.

'Fatal Event', *The Belfast News-letter*, 09/08/1833.

'Fermanagh Man's Shocking Death', *Fermanagh Herald*, 24/05/1930.

Hegarty, Daniel & Hickey, Brian, 1996, 'The Famine Graveyard on Carr's Hill near Cork', *Journal of the Cork Historical and Archaeological Society*, 101, pp. 9–14.

'Pithy Provincial News: Leinster', *Irish Independent*, 23/08/1923.

'Miscellaneous News', *Leinster Express*, 18/10/1851.

'Northern Tragedy', *The Cork Examiner*, 20/05/1930.

O'Sullivan, Muiris & Downey, Liam, 2005, 'Lime Kilns', (19)2 Archaeology Ireland, pp. 18–22.

'Roslea Man's Tragic End', *The Anglo-Celt*, 03/02/1917.

Rynne, Colin, 2001, 'Stone, Brick and Mortar', *Journal of the Cork Historical and Archaeological Society*, 106, pp. 167–174.

Rynne, Colin, 2015, *Industrial Ireland: An Archaeology*, pp. 157–160.

Thackeray, W.M., 1843, *The Irish Sketch Book*, pp. 57, 359.

'Sad Fatality Near Dungannon: Man Falls Into a Limekiln', *The Belfast News-letter*, 19/10/1915.

'The Munster Brick and Lime-Burning Company', *The Freeman's Journal*, 20/06/1873.

The National Folklore Collection, University College Dublin, The Main Manuscript Collection.

The National Folklore Collection, University College Dublin, The Schools' Collection.

Tully Cross Guild Irish Countrywomen's Association, 1985, *Portrait of a Parish: Ballynakill, Connemara*, p. 104.

Welsh, J., 2011, 'Survey of Lime Kiln at Murlough Bay, County Antrim, UAS/09/03', *Ulster Archaeological Society*.

'Wexford Boy Killed', *The Freeman's Journal*, 24/08/1923.

Milling

Aalen, F. H. A., Whelan, K. & Stout, M., 2011, *Atlas of the Irish Rural Landscape* (second edition), pp. 312–314.

Anderson, R. H., 1938, 'The Technical Ancestry of Grain-Milling Devices', *Agricultural History*, 12(3), pp. 256–270.

Bennett, Richard and Elton, John, 1898, *History of Corn Milling, Handstones, Slave and Cattle Mills*, pp. 20–22, 29–31, 72–75.

Binchy, D. A., 1955, 'Irish Law Tracts Re-Edited', *Ériu*, 17, pp. 52–85.

C., 1836, 'Ancient Irish Hand-Mill, or Quern', *The Dublin Penny Journal*, 4(193), pp. 295–296.

Cork County Council Heritage Unit, 2019, *Industrial Heritage of County Cork*.

Department of the Environment, Climate and Communications (Government of Ireland), Geological Survey, The Geological Heritage of Wexford, County Geological Site Report, Harrylock Bay.

Dolan, B., 2012, '"Mysterious waifs of time": some thoughts on the functions of Irish bullaun stones', *The Journal of the Royal Society of Antiquaries of Ireland*, 142/143, pp. 42–58.

Ffrench, J. F. M., 1892, 'St. Mullins, Co. Carlow', *The Journal of the Royal Society of Antiquaries of Ireland*, 2(4), pp. 377–388.

Geaney, M., 2016, 'Timber bridges in medieval Ireland', *The Journal of Irish Archaeology*, 25, pp. 89–104.

Ireland's Holy Wells County-by-County, 2024, St Moling's Well.

Manning, C., 1999, 'Heritage Guide No. 5: St Mullin's: An early ecclesiastical site and medieval Settlement in County Carlow', *Archaeology Ireland*.

Meehan, Joseph B., 1923, 'The Common Quern', *Breifny Antiquarian Society Journal*, II(1), pp. 50–56.

Meehan, Joseph B., 1923, 'The Common Quern', *Breifny Antiquarian Society Journal*, II(1), pp. 50–56.

Price, L., 1959, 'Rock-Basins, or "Bullauns", at Glendalough and Elsewhere', *The Journal of the Royal Society of Antiquaries of Ireland*, 89(2), pp. 161–188.

Rynne, Colin, 2015, *Industrial Ireland: An Archaeology*, pp. 30–44, 161, 194–199.

'The Fatal Mill Accident', *The Cork Examiner*, 08/04/1874.

The National Folklore Collection, University College Dublin, The Main Manuscript Collection.

The National Folklore Collection, University College Dublin, The Schools' Collection.

Iron

Boate, Gerard, 1726, *A Natural History of Ireland, in Three Parts*, pp. 72–76.

Bog Iron's Journal, 2023, 'What is this oily film, and rusty, slimy stuff in swampy areas?', inaturalist.org.

Clancy, E. & Forde Patrick J., 1980, *Ballinaglera Parish, Co. Leitrim: Aspects of Its History and Traditions*, pp. 35–36.

Department of Housing, Local Government and Heritage, National Monuments Service, Hut site: Glebe (Muskerry West By., Ballyvourney Par.), CO058-034001, Historic Environment Viewer.

Dromahair Heritage, Creevelea Ironworks Ancient Ironworks, dromahairheritage.wordpress.com

Government of Ireland, 2009, *Iron: The Repair of Wrought and Cast Ironwork*.

'The Workers and Industry', *Irish Opinion*, 08/12/1917.

Kane M.D., Robert, 1845, *The Industrial Resources of Ireland, Second Edition*.

'Our Coal and Iron Fields', *Leitrim Observer*, 27/04/1935.

McCracken, E. 1957, 'Charcoal-Burning Ironworks in Seventeenth and Eighteenth Century Ireland', *Ulster Journal of Archaeology*, 20, pp. 123–138.

O'Kelly, Michael J., 1952, 'St Gobnait's House, Ballyvourney, Co. Cork', *Journal of the Cork Historical and Archaeological Society*, 57(185), pp. 18–40.

Rondelez, Dr. P., 2018, 'The Irish bowl furnace: origin, history and demise', *Journal of Irish Archaeology*, XXVI, pp. 101–116.

Rondelez, Dr P., 2016, The Sliabh Aughty Furnace Project, *Sliabh Aughty*, no. 16, pp. 2–8.

Rynne, Colin, 2015, *Industrial Ireland: An Archaeology*, pp. 105–128.

Smith, C., 1756, *The Antient and Present State of the County of Kerry*, pp. 94, 102.

'Some Irish Iron Mines Three Centuries Ago', *Irish Independent*, 23/02/1939.

'The Destruction of our Forests – By Whom?', *Honesty Newspaper*, 24/12/1927.

The National Folklore Collection, University College Dublin, The Main Manuscript Collection.
The National Folklore Collection, University College Dublin, The Schools' Collection.
Wallace, A. and Anguilano, L., 2010, 'Iron-smelting and smithing: new evidence emerging on Irish Road Schemes', *Creative Minds. Archaeology and National Roads Authority Monograph Series* no. 7.
Watson, Steven A., 'The System of a Blast Furnace', *Medieval Technology and American History*, engr.psu.edu.
'When Iron Furnaces were Aglow In Connacht', *Irish Press*, 23/03/1933.

THE FUN OF THE FAIR
The Fair Day
'Church of the Sacred Heart, Donnybrook', *The Freeman's Journal*, 1866.
Danaher, Kevin, 2023 (first published 1972), *The Year in Ireland, Irish Calendar Customs*. p. 153.
Dictionary of Irish Biography, Young Henry, dib.ie.
Evans, E. Estyn, 1957 (republished 2000), *Irish Folk Ways*, p. 261.
Hall, Mr. & Mrs. S. C., 1840, *Hall's Ireland:, Mr. and Mrs. Hall's Tour of Ireland 1840*, condensed edition 1984, 2, pp. 294–295.
Joyce, Weston St. John, 1921, *The Neighbourhood of Dublin, Its Topography, Antiquity and Historical Associations*, pp. 76, 272.
'Leenane Fair or "Pattern"', *The Connaught-Telegraph*, 26/08/1876.
Moloney, Eileen, 2024, *Times Were Different Then (Fair Day)*, p. 55.

Oxford English Dictionary, Donnybrook, oed.com.
UK Parliament, 1856, 'Fairs and Markets in Ireland', 29 April 1856, Vol. 141 cc1696-701, api.parliament.uk.
Pegum, Colette, 2016, *The Church of the Sacred Heart Donnybrook 150th Anniversary*.
The National Folklore Collection, University College Dublin, The Main Manuscript Collection.
The National Folklore Collection, University College Dublin, The Schools' Collection.
Thom, Alexander, 1844, 'Fairs Now Held in Ireland', *Thom's Directory*, pp. 645–653.
Tutty, Michael J., 1973, 'Finglas', *Dublin Historical Record*, 26(2), 1973, pp. 66–73.
Wilde, W. R., 1852, *Irish Popular Superstitions*, pp. 17–50.

The Pattern Day
Archdiocese of Tuam, Máméan, 2024, tuamarchdiocese.org.
Clarke, Amanda, Holy Wells of Cork & Kerry, 'Pilgrimage, Partying & Paying the Rounds', holywellscorkandkerry.com.
Crofton Croker, T., 1824, *Researches in the South of Ireland: Illustrative of the Scenery, Architectural Remains, and the Manners and Superstitions of the Peasantry*, pp. 275–283.
Danaher, Kevin, 2023 (first published 1972), *The Year in Ireland, Irish Calendar Customs*, pp. 14, 127, 172–174.
Government of Ireland, Mám Éan (information sign at site).
Ireland's Folklore and Traditions, 'Fairies and Fairy Lore: The reality of the Irish Fairy', irishfolklore.wordpress.com.

Joyce, Weston St. John, 1921, *The Neighbourhood of Dublin, Its Topography, Antiquity and Historical Associations*, pp. 340–341.

Ó Diarmada, Micheál, 2024, interview recorded by folklore collector Anne-Karoline Distel, 'St Moling's Well, Mullenakill, St Albert's Well, Lukeswell', Wikimedia commons.

O'Dwyer, John G., 2017, *Pilgrim Paths of Ireland, From Slieve Mish to Skellig Michael: a guide*, pp. 52–57, 130–136.

O'Sullivan, M., & Downey, L., 2006, 'Holy Wells', *Archaeology Ireland*, 20(1), pp. 35–37.

Rounds at Gougane Barra (information sign at site).

St. Brigid's Shrine – Faughart, 'Stations of St. Brigid's Stream Part Two' (information sign at site).

'St. Lassair's Holy Well, Kilronan', *Leitrim Observer*, 21/10/1967.

The National Folklore Collection, University College Dublin, The Main Manuscript Collection.

The National Folklore Collection, University College Dublin, The Schools' Collection.

Wilde, W. R., 1852, *Irish Popular Superstitions*, pp. 17–50.

Willis, N.P. and Coyne, J. Stirling, 1842, *The Scenery and Antiquities of Ireland*, pp. 82–85.

Faction Fighting

'A Sanguinary Faction Fight in Killarney', *The Kerry Evening Post*, 11/01/1888.

'Another Faction Fight', *The Belfast News-letter*, 11/07/1878.

Carleton, W., 1869 (Tenth Complete Edition), *Traits and Stories of the Irish Peasantry*.

Clancy, E. & Forde Patrick J., 1980, *Ballinaglera Parish, Co. Leitrim: Aspects of Its History and Traditions*, p. 148.

Danaher, Kevin, 1964, *In Ireland Long Ago, The Faction Fighters*, pp. 148–153.

De Latocnaye, Chevalier, 1797 (translated by John Stevenson, 1917), *A Frenchman's Walk through Ireland*.

Department of Housing, Local Government and Heritage, National Monuments Service, Ritual site – holy well: Glebe (Muskerry West By., Ballyvourney Par.), CO058-034009.

'Dreadful Occurrence', *The Belfast News-letter*, 11/07/1834.

'Faction Fight at a Fair', *The Belfast News-letter*, 28/05/1883.

'Faction Fight in Mayo', *The Cork Examiner*, 17/06/1880.

'Faction Fight in the County Limerick', Carlow Morning Post, 12/06/1875.

'Faction Fight in the South of Ireland', *The Belfast News-letter*, 20/09/1850.

'Faction Fight Near Galway, A Man Killed', *The Belfast News-letter*, 19/02/1891.

'Faction Fight', *The Belfast News-letter*, 11/07/1834.

'Faction Fighting at Ballyvourney', *The Cork Examiner*, 18/06/1896.

'Faction Fighting', 2024, Historical Wexford (Facebook page).

'Faction Fighting', *The Kerry Evening Post*, 31/12/1845.

'Faction Fighting', *The Pictorial Times Newspaper*, 1846.

'Fatal Faction Fight', *Eagle and County Cork Advertiser*, 21/02/1891.

Fortune, Michael, 2023, 'Faction Fighting at Moneyhore', Folklore.ie (Facebook page).

Hall, Mr & Mrs. S. C., 1846, *Ireland: Its Scenery, Character, &c., Vol. 1, A New Edition*, pp. 428–435.

Horgan, Donal, 1988, *Echo After Echo: Killarney and Its History*, p. 42.

Hurley, J., 2010, *Irish Gangs and Stick-Fighting: In the Works of William Carleton* (second edition).

'Irish Nationalist Faction Fights', *The Leinster Express*, 21/09/1895.

Joyce, P.W., 1910, 'Clehalpeen', 'Shillelah', *English As We Speak It In Ireland*, pp. 235, 321.

'Kilkenny', Finns Leinster Journal, 08/12/1802.

'King's County – Faction Fight and Riot at a Fair', *The Cork Examiner*, 27/03/1857.

'Limerick Faction Fights' (a retrospective article), *Limerick Leader*, 16/08/1912.

Na Chéad Fight Clubs (documentary), TG4.

National Archives, Chief Secretary's Office Registered Papers, 1828 Outrage Reports, Report on a murder at a riot at Moneyhore Fair, CSO/RP/OR/1828/277.

National Museum of Ireland, 2024, 19th Century Faction Fighting, museum.ie.

O'Donnell, P., 1975, *The Irish Faction Fighters of the 19th Century*.

Pegum, Colette, 2016, *The Church of the Sacred Heart Donnybrook 150th Anniversary*.

'Rides Through the County of Cork – The Priest's Fireside', *Dublin Penny Journal*, 21/01/1835.

'Terrible Faction Fight Near Newpallas', *The Cork Examiner*, 14/07/1882.

'The Ballinhassig Massacre, Meeting of the Citizens', *The Cork Examiner*, 30/7/1845.

'The Faction Fight', *The Belfast News-letter*, 09/04/1847.

'The Faction Fight', *The Pictorial Times*, 17/02/1844.

'Before the Right Hon. Lord Norbury', *The Freeman's Journal*, 09/08/1814.

'Kilkenny–Saturday, August 6', *The Moderator*, 06/08/1814.

NFC, T0088.5, E.L., Rathmore, Co. Cork.

NFC, T0270.3, P.W., Blackstick, Co. Louth.

The National Folklore Collection, University College Dublin, The Main Manuscript Collection.

The National Folklore Collection, University College Dublin, The Schools' Collection.

'The Result of Boycotting, Serious Faction Fight', *The Belfast News-letter*, 18/05/1887.

Waterford Mail, 02/04/1828.

PASTIMES
Handball

Aalen, F. H. A., Whelan, K. & Stout, M., 2011, *Atlas of the Irish Rural Landscape* (second edition), pp. 248–249.

Crofton Croker, T., 1824, *Researches in the South of Ireland*, p. 133.

Cronin, Mike, Murphy, William and Paul Rouse (eds.), 2009, *The Gaelic Athletic Association 1884–2009*, pp. 20, 71–73, 222–225.

'Desecration of the Sabbath', *Leinster Express (Mercantile and Agricultural Advertiser)*, 09/09/1843.

Gilleece, Emma, 2022, '100 Buildings: A Monaghan handball alley, an unsung monument to Ireland's past', RTÉ.

'Handball Match', *The Freeman's Journal*, 13/08/1886.

'Handball', *The Cork Examiner*, 29/07/1895.

Herihy, M. (Ed.), 2003, *Ordnance Survey Letters: Kilkenny*, p. 94.

Kavanagh, Joan, 2020, 'Chronology of the Important Events during the 1798 Rebellion in County Wicklow', heritage.wicklowheritage.org.

'Louth and the Failure of the 1798 Rebellion', *Irish Independent*, 06/02/2004, independent.ie.

McElligott, Tom, 1984, *The Game, The Players, The History*.

Murphy, Sean (Ed.), 1984, *A History of Handball in Munster 1884–1994*.

O'Connor, Tom, 2010, 'Handball – A Brief History', gaahandball.ie.

O'Halloran, Kenneth, 2014, 'Three Walls in Search of a Ball', *The New York Times Magazine*.

O'Sullivan, M., & Downey, L., 2017, 'Gaelic Games', *Archaeology Ireland*, 31(3), pp. 25–29.

Ryan, Áine, 'Political Actions at Handball Alleys', irishhandballalley.humap.site.

Ryan, Áine, 'Proto-Alleys at Churchyards', irishhandballalley.humap.site.

Ryan, Áine, 2009, 'Architecture: Handball alleys', historyireland.com.

Ryan, Áine, 2023, 'Saint Patrick's Collect, Maynooth, County Kildare', irishhandballalley.ie.

'Drogheda, 1798', *The Drogheda Independent*, 25/06/1960.

'The Handball Championship, Victory of Fitzgerald', *Kerry News*, 23/08/1895.

The National Folklore Collection, University College Dublin, The Schools' Collection.

'The West Wicklow Massacres', 1798 Rebellion Casualty Database (Facebook group).

University of Galway Archives and Special Collections, 2012, 'A Ban on Ye Small Ball', nuigarchives.blogspot.com

Vigors, P. D., 1893, 'The Antiquities of Ullard, County Kilkenny, 1892', *The Journal of the Royal Society of Antiquaries of Ireland*, 3(3), pp. 251–260.

'Wonderful Escape', *The Belfast News-letter*, 11/03/1828.

Stone Lifting

Carrigan, Rev. William, *The History and Antiquities of the Dioceses of Ossory*, pp. 354-357.

Clancy, E. & Forde Patrick J., 1980, *Ballinaglera Parish, Co. Leitrim: Aspects of Its History and Traditions*, p. 152.

Department of Housing, Heritage and Local Government, 'Church: Church Island', National Monuments Service, Historic Environment Viewer (ArcGIS Online).

Department of Housing, Heritage and Local Government, 'Churchclara', National Monuments Service, Historic Environment Viewer (ArcGIS Online).

Disert Graveyard (information sign at site).

NFCS, 0224, 404, P. O'Rourke, Ballinamore, Co. Leitrim.

Nolan, D., & Heffernan, C., 2025, 'Tests of Manhood: Uncovering the History and Popularity of Stone Lifting in Ireland', *Irish Economic and Social History*.

O'Flaherty, Liam, 1929, *The Mountain Tavern and Other Stories,* 'The Stone', pp. 234–242.

Pilgrimage In Medieval Ireland, 2013, 'Saint Colmcille's Well Disert Donegal', pilgrimagemedievalireland.com.

The National Folklore Collection, University College Dublin, The Schools' Collection.

CURES

Stones

'After Twelve Centuries St. Lasair Has Not Been Forgotten', *Roscommon Herald*, 11/07/1986.

Aghade Holed Stone, Duchas, The Heritage Service, 2024, (information sign at site).

'Alt a Dubháin (Altadaven), Impressions of a Visitor', *Strabane Chronicle*, 31/07/1915.

Altadaven, The Story of the Chair and Well (information sign at site).

'Beautiful area Aughers well for an enjoyable hike', *Belfast Telegraph*, 06/12/2008.

Bigger, F. J., 1898, 'The Lake and Church of Kilmakilloge, the Ancient Church, Holy Well, and Bullán-Stone of Temple Feaghna, and the Holy Well and Shrine at Saint Finan's, County Kerry', *The Journal of the Royal Society of Antiquaries of Ireland*, 8(4), pp. 314–324.

Danaher, Kevin, 1964, *Gentle Places and Simple Things*, p. 88.

Department of Housing, Local Government and Heritage, National Monuments Service.

Department of Housing, Local Government and Heritage, National Monuments Service, Bullaun Stone: Garranes, KE102-038003, Historic Environment Viewer.

Department of the Environment, Climate and Communications (Government of Ireland), Geological Survey Ireland, Louth – County Geological Site Report.

Dolan, J. T., & J. M. D., 1904, 'The Early Legends of Louth', *Journal of the County Louth Archaeological Society*, 1(1), p. 19.

Hall, Mr & Mrs. S. C., 1846, *Ireland: Its Scenery, Character, &c., Vol. 1, A New Edition,* pp. 121-122.

'History of Bonane', Bonane Heritage Park, 2007, bonaneheritagepark.com.

Ireland's Holy Wells County-by-County, 2024, St. MacCullin's Well (Grallagh), ihwcbc.omeka.net.

Kelly, Brendan, 'Myths, Madness and Insane Ears: Making Sense of the History of Psychiatry in Ireland', *History Ireland*, historyireland.com.

'New Cross at St. Lasair Well', *Roscommon Herald*, 26/09/1975.

NFCS, 0959, 302

'O'Carolan Harp Festival Opening on Sunday', *Leitrim Observer*, 30/07/1988.

O'Donovan, J., 1839, *Ordnance Survey Letters: Carlow*, pp. 403–404.

O'Kearney, Nicholas, 1852, 'Folklore'. *Transactions of the Kilkenny Archaeological Society*, 2(1), p. 35.

Ryan, John, 1833, *The History and Antiquities of the County of Carlow*, pp. 19, 338.

'Saint Lasair's Holy Well Stations', 1983 (information sign at site, noted with prayers approved by Bishop of Ardagh and Clonmacnois) .

'Saint Patrick's Chair and Well', Voices from the Dawn, voicesfromthedawn.com.

Shine, Father John, 1992, *Bonane: Saint Feaghna*, pp. 30–39.

Tait, Clodagh, 2002, *Death, Burial and Commemoration in Ireland, 1550–1650*, p. 111.

The National Folklore Collection, University College Dublin, The Main Manuscript Collection.

The National Folklore Collection, University College Dublin, The Schools' Collection.

'The Rolls of Butter', Bonane Heritage Park, bonaneheritagepark.com.

Wood-Martin, W. G., 1888, '"Holed-Stone" in the County Carlow', *The Journal of the Royal Historical and Archaeological Association of Ireland*, 8(76), pp. 471–472.

Water

Branigan, Gary, 2012, *Ancient and Holy Wells of Dublin*, p. 46.

Clancy, E. & Forde Patrick J., 1980, *Ballinaglera Parish, Co. Leitrim: Aspects of Its History and Traditions*, p. 7.

Clarke, Amanda, 'Tobar Mhuire, Lady's Well, Titeskin', pilgrimagemedievalireland.com.

Conneely, Jacob, 2024, 'A Brief History of St. Augustine's Well', galwaycivictrust.ie.

Crofton Croker, T., *Researches in the South of Ireland, 1824*, pp. 275–283.

Danaher, Kevin, 2023 (first published 1972), *The Year in Ireland: Irish Calendar Customs*, pp. 113, 180.

'Discovery of a Chalybeate Spa of Very Valuable Properties Near Trim', *The Freeman's Journal*, 22/01/1842.

Doyle, Helen, 'St Moling's Well', Ireland's Holy Wells County-by-County, ihwcbc.omeka.net

E. K., 1919, 'The Boyne and What It Stands For', *The Irish Monthly*, 47(557), pp.595–598.

Ffrench, J. F. M., 1892, 'St. Mullins, Co. Carlow', *The Journal of the Royal Society of Antiquaries of Ireland*, 2(4), pp. 377–388.

Gleann na nGealt, 2012, TG4, (documentary).

Ireland's Holy Wells County-by-County, 2024

Joyce, Patrick Joseph, 1910, *A Forgotten Part of Ireland*, pp. 120–127

Kenny, Tom, 2024, interview by Manchán Magan, *Ag Triall ar an Tobar* (documentary), 'Saint Augustine's Well'.

Neill, K., 1993, 'The Broighter Hoard: Or How Carson Caught the Boat', *Archaeology Ireland*, 7(2), pp. 24–26.

O Connor, Brigid, 'Tobar na nGealt,' Ireland's Holy Wells County-by-County, ihwcbc.omeka.ne

Ó Diarmada, Micheál, 2024, interview recorded by folklore collector Anne-Karoline Distel, Wikimedia commons.

O'Donovan, John, 1841, *Ordnance Survey Letters: Kerry*. O'Dowd, P., 2008, 'Holy Wells of Galway City', *Journal of the Galway Archaeological and Historical Society*, 60, pp. 136–153.

O'Sullivan, M., & Downey, L., 2006, 'Holy Wells', *Archaeology Ireland*, 20(1), pp. 35–37.

O'Sullivan, Sean, 1974, *The Folklore of Ireland*, p. 113.

'Our Ancient Landscapes. Holy Wells in Ireland', The Heritage Council, 2023, www.heritagecouncil.ie.

'Our Lady's Well, Near Cloyne', Holy Wells of Cork and Kerry, 2016, holywellscorkandkerry.com

'Our Parish: Ballinaglera', Ballinaglera Parish Website, ballinaglera.org.

Ryan, Salvador (ed.), 2016, 'The Black Death in Kilkenny' *Death and the Irish: a miscellany*, (Bernadette Williams), p. 39.

Selling, Kim, 1998, 'The Locus of the Sacred in the Celtic Otherworld', *Sydney Open Journals*.

Smith, Charles, 1893, *The Ancient and Present State of the County and City of Cork*, p. 118.

St Moling's Pilgrim's Route, Ireland's National Inventory of Intangible Cultural Heritage, nationalinventoryich.tcagsm.gov.ie.

The National Folklore Collection, University College Dublin, The Main Manuscript Collection.

The National Folklore Collection, University College Dublin, The Schools' Collection.

Uí Chaoimh, Mary Jo, 2024, interview by Manchan Magan, Tobar Naomh Damhnait (Saint Dymphna's Holy Well), *Ag Triall ar an Tobar* (documentary).

'Women, Water and Wisdom in Celtic Mythology', Heritage Ireland (Shauna Fox), heritageireland.ie

Trees

'A Story of Discovery: Natural Compound Helps Treat Breast and Ovarian Cancers', 2015, National Cancer Institute, www.cancer.gov.

Danaher, Kevin, 1964, *Gentle Places and Simple Things*, pp. 67–72.

Danaher, Kevin, 2023 (first published 1972), *The Year in Ireland: Irish Calendar Customs*, pp. 86–127.

Fortune, Michael, 2023, *The Folklore of Wexford*, pp. 74, 81, 32–35.

Holy Wells of Cork and Kerry, holywellscorkandkerry.com.

Irish Tree Explorers Network (UCC), 'Euonymous Eoropaeus', ucc.ie/en/tree-explorers

Kelly, Fergus, 1999, *Trees in Early Ireland*.

McKillop, James, 1998, *A Dictionary of Celtic Mythology*.

Millea, Sam, 2024, folklore collected by Deirdre O'Neill, 19/10/2024.

NFCS, 0910, 104, Garret Sinnott, (56), Ardattin, Co. Carlow

Ó Diarmada, Micheál, 2024, folklore collected by Anne-Karoline Distel, Wikimedia commons.

O'Sullivan, M., & Downey, L., 2022. Assembly sites in medieval Ireland. Archaeology Ireland, 36(2), pp. 40-44.

'Sacred Trees in Ancient Ireland', irisharchaeology.ie.

The Heritage Council, 2023, Our Ancient Landscapes, Holy Wells in Ireland. heritagecouncil.ie

The National Folklore Collection, University College Dublin, The Main Manuscript Collection

The National Folklore Collection, University College Dublin, The Schools' Collection

Blessed Clay

'A Famous Graveyard', *Irish Press*, 22/04/1946.

'After Twelve Centuries St. Lasair Has Not Been Forgotten', *Roscommon Herald*, 11/07/1986.

'Saint Colmcille's Well Disert Donegal', 2013, pilgrimagemedievalireland.com

'Soil From a Northern Ireland Graveyard May Lead Scientists to a Powerful New Antibiotic', 2020, *Smithsonian Magazine*, www.smithsonianmag.com.

Butler, Isaac, 1892, A Journey to Lough Derg circa. 1749, Journal of the Royal Society of Antiquaries of Ireland, pp. 22, 13–24, 126–36 (St. Sechnall's Well)

Clancy, E. & Forde Patrick J., 1980, *Ballinaglera Parish, Co. Leitrim: Aspects of Its History and Traditions*, p. 32

ClanDonnell (David McDonnell), 2020, The Magical Dirt of Boho Fermanagh, clandonnell.net

Crofton Croker, T., 1824, Researches in the South of Ireland: Illustrative of the Scenery, Architectural Remains, and the Manners and Superstitions of the Peasantry, p. 170

Department of Housing, Local Government and Heritage, National Monuments Service, Ritual Site – Holy Well: Bonestown (St. Sechnall's Well), Historic Environment Viewer

Fortune, Michael, 2024, Folklore.ie on Facebook, Gartan Clay from Donegal

Hall, Mr and Mrs. S.C., 1846, *Ireland: Its Scenery, Character, &c., Vol. 1, A New Edition*, pp. 283–285

'Healing Medicine ... Boho Soil Showing Cures For Ailments', *Fermanagh Herald*, 03/03/2021.

Ireland's Holy Wells, County-by-County, St Moling's Well, ihwcbc.omeka.net.

Irish Folklore and Traditions, Saint Declan's Pattern Day, irishfolklore.wordpress.com.

Keadue Local Area Site, St. Lasair's Holy Well, keadue.net.

'Kell Board of Guardians,' *Meath Chronicle*, 09/01/1904.

Mooney, James, 1888, The Funeral Customs of Ireland, pp. 287, 291.

NFCS, 0179, 032

Ó Diarmada, Micheál, 2024, Interview recorded by folklore collector Anne-Karoline Distel, Wikimedia commons.

Ridge, Anne, 2009, *Death Customs in Rural Ireland: Traditional Funerary Rites in the Irish Midlands*, p. 93–94

Sacred Heart Church Cemetery, Boho, County Fermanagh (information sign at site).

Sacred Landscapes, Kilcummin (Cill Chuimín – Cuimíns Church), sacredlandscapes.ie.

The National Folklore Collection, University College Dublin, The Main Manuscript Collection .

The National Folklore Collection, University College Dublin, The Schools' Collection.

'To the People of Ireland – Letter IV', *The Nenagh Guardian*, 15/02/1843.

'St. Lassair's Holy Well – An Appeal', *Roscommon Herald*, 16/02/1968.

'The Burial of the Poor', *The Freeman's Journal*, 15/03/1870.

'New Cross at St. Lasair Well', *Roscommon Herald*, 26/09/1975.

Sweathouses

Ballinaglera Parish Website, 'Our Parish: Ballinaglera', ballinaglera.org.

Clancy, E. & Forde Patrick J., 1980, *Ballinaglera Parish, Co. Leitrim: Aspects of Its History and Traditions*, p. 163.

De Latocnaye, Chevalier, 1797 (translated by John Stevenson, 1917), *A Frenchman's Walk through Ireland*, p. 92

Evans, E. Estyn, 1961, *Irish Folk Ways*, pp. 124–125.

Group of the Study of Irish Historical Settlement, 1970, Bulletin No.1, Investigation of a Sweathouse near Hollyford, County Tipperary, p. 36.

Harte, Aidan, 2010, 'The Munster Sweathouse Project', *North Munster Antiquarian Journal*, 50, p. 77.

Kearns, Katie &Ylimaunu, Timo, 2021, *The Sweathouses of Ireland: The Disappeared Folk Tradition of Sweat Bathing*.

Kearns, Katie, 2016, *Understanding Sweathouses in Ireland with special reference to County Leitrim*.

NFCS, 0208, 248, Joseph Rourke (74), Shancurry, Co. Leitrim, 1937

'Our Ancestors Sweated Away Their Aches', *Irish Press*, 31/01/1968.

'Sweat-House Located in Co. Tipperary', *The Cork Examiner*, 02/07/1970.

The Fr. Michael O'Flanagan History & Heritage Centre, Inishmurray, Co Sligo, carrowkeel.com.

The National Folklore Collection, University College Dublin, The Schools' Collection.

Wakeman, W.F., 1893, *A Survey of the Antiquarian Remains on the Island of Inismurray*, pp. xi, 37.

DEATH
The Wake/The Burial/Keening/Undertakers/Memorials

'Ancient Customs: The Crusheens', mayo.ie.

Carleton, William, 1869, *Traits and Stories of the Irish Peasantry, Party Fight and Funeral*, (Tenth Complete Edition).

Colfer, Billy, 2008, *Wexford: A Town and Its Landscape*.

Crofton Croker, T., 1823, *Researches in the South of Ireland: Illustrative of the Scenery, Architectural Remains, and the Manners and Superstitions of the Peasantry*, pp. 166-184

Danaher, Kevin, 1964, *In Ireland Long Ago*, pp. 64–71, 169–188

De Latocnaye, Chevalier, 1797 (translated by John Stevenson, 1917), *A Frenchman's Walk through Ireland*.

Fahy, J.A., 1986, *The Glory of Cong*, pp. 19–20

Fortune, Michael, 2023, *The Folklore of Wexford Volume 1: Living Folklore, Traditions, Stories and Calendar Customs*.

Harrington, Aiden, County Clare Heritage Office, Fenloe Church and Graveyard – A Layperson's Guide, heritage.clareheritage.org.

Hitchcock, R., 1852, 'Gleanings from Country Church-Yards'. *Transactions of the Kilkenny Archaeological Society*, 2(1), pp. 127–133.

J. H. "Ancient Funeral Custom in Kilmore Parish." The Past: The Organ of the Uí Cinsealaigh Historical Society, no. 3, 1925, pp. 41–46.

Maxwell, W.H., 1915, *Wild Sports of the West*, pp. 184–185.

Millea, Sam, Kyleva Monuments, Kilkenny 2024, Folklore collected by Deirdre O'Neill.

Mooney, James, 1888, *The Funeral Customs of Ireland*, pp. 268–296.

Mulvey, Con (ed.), 1998, *The Memorial Inscriptions and Related History of Kiltullagh, Killimordaly and Esker Graveyards*, p. 2.

Navan Historical Society, 2011, Market Square, navanhistory.ie.

Nic Néill, M., 1946, 'Wayside Death Cairns in Ireland', *Béaloideas*, 16(1/2), pp. 49–63.

Nicholson, Asenath, 1847, *Ireland's Welcome to the Stranger; or An excursion through Ireland, in 1844 & 1845, for the purpose of personally investigating the condition of the poor*, pp. 62, 306.

NFCS, 0877, 134, Thomas Doyle (53), Ballask, Kilmore, Co. Wexford

O'G., *Dublin Penny Journal*, 26/01/1833, 1(31).

O'Dowd, P., 1998, 'Leachta Cuimhne or Funerary Cairns of Wormhole, Moycullen, Co. Galway', *Journal of the Galway Archaeological and Historical Society*, 50, pp.201–209.

O'Regan, William, 1817, *Memoirs of the Legal, Literary, and Political Life of the Late The Right Honourable John Philpot Curran*, p. 5.

Ridge, Anne, 2009, *Death Customs in Rural Ireland: Traditional Funerary Rites in the Irish Midlands*.

Ryan, Salvador, (ed.), 2016, *Death and the Irish: a miscellany*.

Tait, Clodagh, 2002, *Death, Burial and Commemoration in Ireland 1550-1650*.

The National Folklore Collection, University College Dublin, The Main Manuscript Collection.

The National Folklore Collection, University College Dublin, The Schools' Collection.

Tully Cross Guild Irish Countrywomen's Association, 1985, *Portrait of a Parish: Ballynakill, Connemara*, p. 9.

Whitney, S., 2019, 'The Irish tobacco business 1779-1935', hdl.handle.net.

AFTERWORD

Synge, John M., 1912, *The Aran Islands, Part III and IV*, p. 13.

ACKNOWLEDGEMENTS

The assistance and co-operation of the following is acknowledged with thanks:

- Bruff Tidy Towns
- Church of Ireland Diocese of Kilmore, Elphin and Ardagh
- Dept. of Housing, Local Government and Heritage, Ireland
- John Devereux
- Anne-Karoline Distel
- Andrew Doherty
- Michael Fortune
- Gill Books – the wonderful team including Isabelle Hanrahan, Patrick O'Donoghue, Iollann Ó Murchú, Charlie Lawlor, Padraig McCormack and Jane Rogers
- Christy Hussey
- Brian Kennedy, Glenview Folk Museum, Ballinamore, County Leitrim
- David Keohane
- Paul Maguire
- Sam Millea
- Philip Moody
- Vincent (Jasper) Murphy, McCarthy's Fethard
- The National Folklore Collection, UCD
- National Library of Ireland
- National Monuments Service
- National Museums of Ireland
- National Museums NI
- Barry O'Carroll
- Seán Ó Coistealbha
- The co-operation of the Office of Public Works and the Department of Housing, Local Government and Heritage for photography at Parke Castle is acknowledged.

- Micheál Ó Goill
- Paul Rondelez
- Joan Russell
- Trinity College Dublin
- Wicklow Gaol

For more information on the Remnants of our Past project, see:
Instagram: @remnantsofourpast · Tiktok: @remnantsofourpast
YouTube: @remnantsofourpast · Website: www.remnantsofourpast.com